BER

DISNEYLAND
and the Theme Parks

- A <V> in the text denotes a highly recommended sight
- A complete A–Z of practical information starts on p.113
- Extensive mapping throughout: on cover flaps and in text

Printed in Switzerland by Weber SA, Bienne.

1st edition (1995/1996)

The author, researchers and publishers of this guide declare that they are
independent of Disneyland and all other members of the Disney corporate
family. The material described in this guide has not been approved in any
manner by the Disney organization. Within this guide, no attempt has been
made by the author or publisher to infringe copyrights or trademarks of the
Walt Disney Company Inc. such as *Audio-Animatronics*™ and *Captain
EO*™, which have been presented only in those contexts to which they
legally and properly belong, nor those trademarks and copyrights pending.

**The contents of this publication are believed to be correct at the
time of printing, but changes do occur. Please write to Berlitz with
your comments at one of the above addresses.**

Text:	Fred Mawer
Editor:	Delphine Verroest
Photography:	Fred Mawer, except pp.6, 10, 29 (main pic) 32, 37 and 57 by Donna Dailey; pp.61 (inset), 95 and 96 by Doug Traverso; pp.4, 47 and 49 by Six Flags Magic Mountain; pp.43 and 100 by Universal Studios; p.38 by Wild Rivers.
Layout:	Visual Image
Cartography:	Visual Image
Thanks to:	The theme parks and the Convention and Visitors Bureaux of Los Angeles, Anaheim and San Diego

Cover photograph: *Montezooma's Revenge, Knott's Berry Farm* © Berlitz
Photograph on p.4: *Psyclone ride, Six Flags Magic Mountain*
            © Six Flags Magic Mountain

CONTENTS

Disneyland and the Theme Parks

'A place where dreams come true' may well apply to Southern California as a whole and its theme parks in particular. The most 'Western' of all states has always attracted dreamers in search of the good life, or wishing to make a new start. It isn't difficult to see why: year-round sunshine, vast stretches of golden sand, fertile valleys and other natural riches create a land of endless opportunities. The biggest and most lucrative of them all has proved to be entertainment. This is the movie centre of the world, and it's also a great theme-park haven. Here, one man created Disneyland – 'the happiest place on earth'.

The theme park attractions are inextricably linked to the wider Californian experience. You wouldn't dream of coming to the West coast and not setting foot outside Disneyland. The ever-blue sky and golden beaches pounded by crashing Pacific surf – immortalized by the Beach Boys – entice you to relax, California-style.

Need a change of scenery? Shopping malls whisk you off to Mediterranean courtyards, Mexican plazas and Caribbean islands, while restaurants carry you away to the Old West, an underwater grotto or a Chinese temple. Myths and reality mingle indecipherably in the fantasy worlds of Hollywood, synonymous with moviedom, and Beverly Hills, byword for luxurious living. The San Diegan lifestyle, with beaches, a plethora of museums and a vibrant downtown at hand, seems almost too good to be true.

Of course, some aspects of Southern California bring you back to reality with a bump. Avoid spending too much time around Disneyland, in the large grid of modern development that constitutes urban Orange County. In sprawling Los Angeles, gridlocked traffic, pollution and housing problems are taking their toll, with the possibility of violence and racial conflicts adding to the tension. **5**

Always at the back of everyone's mind is the 'Big One', particularly after the havoc caused by a serious earthquake in January 1994.

Step back, however, and let the magic work. Youth and energy characterize Southern California, where the search for life in the fast lane is manifest in the proliferation of sports cars on the highways. There's simply so much to enjoy that you may never have time to pause, let alone worry.

To find entertainment on a grand scale, you need look no further than the theme parks. Your biggest problem will be picking a favourite from such diverse attractions as hair-raising Magic Mountain, magical Disneyland or the fascinating wildlife parks of San Diego.

Disneyland may be second in the pecking order to its younger sister Disneyworld in Orlando, Florida, but the zestful, daily performance of its cast is just as good and the animation of its attractions just as professional – in fact, the latest technological wonders often feature here first. Disneyland may be California's smallest theme park, but it boasts by far the largest concentration of attractions, and is the only one that demands more than a day to enjoy fully.

*F*un on the sand – the beach is just a stone's throw from most of Southern California's theme parks.

While live performers are limited to the bands and parades in Disneyland, one of the greatest pleasures of **Knott's Berry Farm** lies in meeting the larger-than-life, flesh-and-bone cowboys and blacksmiths in Ghost Town.

Though only a few miles apart, Knott's doesn't attempt to compete with Disneyland. Its home-grown, low-key atmosphere – in stark contrast with the slickness of Disneyland – is part of its charm.

The state-of-the-art rides, shows and special effects of **Universal Studios** hurl you headlong into the late 20th century. In L.A.'s San Fernando Valley, you can get a snapshot of the biggest film studios in the world in action, on the fascinating backlot tram tour.

Six Flags Magic Mountain, now owned by Time Warner, is promoting a film image of its own, too, through Batman and Bugs Bunny themed areas and shows. However, nothing will ever eclipse Magic Mountain's fame as the be-all and end-all roller-coaster park, with no less than eight terrifying runaway rides.

At the wildlife parks in San Diego, the thrills are of an altogether different kind. The painstaking creation of natural habitats at **San Diego Zoo**, the giant landscaped enclosures of **San Diego Wild Animal Park** and the acrobatic shows at **Sea World** make these parks some of the best places in the world to see animals in captivity.

Different though they may be, the parks have one common factor: they all have a lovable character, whether it be fictional – Mickey at Disneyland, Snoopy at Knott's, ET at Universal, Bugs Bunny at Magic Mountain – or real, such as Shamu, Sea World's killer whale, or the koala bears at San Diego Zoo.

What are the secrets to holidaying around this West Coast playground? Let yourself go and soak up the easy-going atmosphere. Most importantly, be sure to experience all of Southern California's diverse pleasures: stroll down Hollywood Boulevard, take in the boardwalk extravaganza at Venice, munch a humble hot dog, dine out on fresh, imaginative California cuisine and, of course, revel in a chance encounter with Mickey Mouse.

*M*aking friends at Disneyland – furry creatures live side by side with cartoon characters.

Theme Park Histories

DISNEYLAND

The world's first theme park was born on 17 July 1955. Built in a year and a day at a cost of $17 million, it was very much Walt Disney's dream: 'I had everything mortgaged including my family', he joked. Few would back the adventure initially, with everyone warning Walt that Disneyland would be 'a Hollywood spectacular ... a spectacular failure'. How wrong they were: Disneyland has received 350 million visitors since it first opened, and registers over 11 million visitors a year. Along with Walt Disney World's Magic Kingdom in Florida, it ranks as the most popular attraction in the United States.

The initial and original 18 attractions, spread across five realms – Main Street, Fantasyland, Frontierland, Tomorrowland and Adventureland – were built on a 160-acre (65ha) orange grove in rural Anaheim. The park has evolved over the years, as new attractions and lands have been added. 1959 heralded the first daily monorail to operate in the US; 1963 saw the birth of *Audio-Animatronics* (see p.13) with the Enchanted Tiki Room; in 1966 New Orleans Square was added (in that same year Walt Disney died; Disneyland was the only park he saw completed); Bear Country (later called Critter Country) was opened in 1972; while the newest land, Mickey's Toontown, sprung up in 1993. WESTCOT – an entirely new $3-billion park with themed global villages, similar in style to Disney World's EPCOT – is planned to arrive around the year 2000.

KNOTT'S BERRY FARM

Berry-growing Walter Knott and his wife Cordelia came to Buena Park in 1920. In little over a decade, Walter Knott had become the undisputed 'Berry King' of the US. However, business really took off in the 1930s, when he began to grow a new strain of berry, the boysenberry. His wife Cordelia provided tea and pie to hungry visitors, and, in 1934, served her first chicken dinners **9**

Ghost Town, the original area of Knott's Berry Farm, leaves the 20th century far behind.

disappeared in 1960. The park only started charging an admission fee in 1968, however.

The latest major section of the park came in 1983, when Snoopy and the Peanuts gang pitched camp (see p.25).

UNIVERSAL STUDIOS

Universal Studios was established in 1912 in tiny offices in New York. The motion picture industry, however, was taking root on the West Coast, where land was cheap, scenic settings plentiful and sunny weather assured throughout the year.

When, in 1914, Carl Laemmle purchased a 130-acre (52ha) chicken ranch in north Hollywood to build a new studio for Universal, the motion picture industry really took off in California. By the 1920s, Hollywood and its vicinity had become the movie-making centre of the world – and has remained so to this day.

on her wedding china. Within weeks, people waited for several hours for Cordelia's delicious dinners and boysenberry pies. These days the restaurant serves 1.5 million chicken dinners a year.

As a diversion for the waiting patrons, in 1940 Walter began building a replica of an Old West town, with buildings relocated from abandoned desert towns, Knott's Berry Farm's Ghost Town.

With the advent of Disneyland in 1955, the Knott family feared for the worst, but Knott's car park was full on the day of its rival's opening. Responding to the competition, the site was gradually developed into an amusement park with rides and arcades, **10** and the last boysenberry field

Universal Studios proved a great attraction right from the very early days. People wanted to see the studios, and soon were being charged 25 cents for a tour of the sets, which allowed them to cheer and jeer as they watched silent movies being made. The theme park proper began in 1964, with a ticket seller, two guides and two tram drivers. The following year, the Entertainment Center was opened with live shows. In 1991, sound stages were converted into more attractions in the Studio Center, and in 1993, Universal City finally acquired its first true street with the opening of the stunning CityWalk (see p.41).

SAN DIEGO ANIMAL PARKS

The story goes that in 1916 a local physician, Dr Harry Wegeforth, on his way home from work, heard the roar of nearby caged lions. The animals were on display at the Panama-California International Exposition, held in San Diego's Balboa Park (see p.91). Turning to his brother, Harry Wegeforth enthused: 'Wouldn't it be splendid if San Diego had a zoo! I think I'll start one.'

From the modest remains of the Exposition, the **San Diego Zoo** has expanded through the years beyond all recognition. It's become increasingly concerned with breeding programmes and conservation. (In 1966, it hosted the world's first conference on the role of zoos in conservation.) Now it's at the forefront of creating near-natural habitats for the zoo's wildlife – the so-called 'bioclimatic zones' (see p.85).

Its 'sister', the **San Diego Wild Animal Park**, opened in 1972. Its purpose was to expand the zoo's breeding capabilities and lessen the zoo's reliance on dwindling stocks of animals from the wild. It was also designed as a tourist attraction to allow the park to be financially self-sufficient.

Sea World marine park has always had conservation in mind ever since it opened in 1964 as part of the development of the aquatic waterpark of San Diego's Mission Bay. Since then, three other Sea Worlds have sprouted in Orlando, Florida; San Antonio, Texas; and Aurora, Ohio.

Where to Go

Southern California's theme parks can be divided up into three separate geographical locations: Orange County, south of Los Angeles (incorporating Disneyland and Knott's Berry Farm); northern L.A. (covering Universal Studios and Magic Mountain); and San Diego (Sea World, San Diego Zoo and San Diego Wild Animal Park).

As Orange County, Los Angeles and San Diego are each major holiday destinations in their own right, you might consider staying put in just one of the three areas. If you intend visiting parks in more than one area, however, it might be wise to stay in each destination.

There's plenty to do outside the theme parks – a Californian beach is always within easy reach, while L.A. and San Diego offer outstanding museums and fascinating neighbourhoods to explore.

Orange County Theme Parks

Orange County, south of Los Angeles, is home to two of the most popular theme parks in Southern California. Disneyland, in Anaheim, is six miles

*G*et set, go! For an action-packed visit, be prepared to cover a lot of ground.

(10km) away from Knott's Berry Farm in Buena Park. Both offer a wealth of attractions in totally different styles.

DISNEYLAND

'Here you leave today and enter the world of yesterday, tomorrow and fantasy,' you're told as you enter The Magic Kingdom. Disneyland's rides are less scary than other parks. Indeed, its rides are accurately billed instead as attractions. What is so seductive about this ultimate escapist utopia, however, is the attention to detail that has gone into its conception. Each of its seven worlds is lovingly crafted, even down to the plants and signs. Staff are called cast members, and they're all expected to contribute a little bit of 'pixiedust' to the daily show.

Be sure to stay until after dark, when a myriad of twinkling lights enhance the land of make-believe to virtual perfection. You'll never do Disneyland justice in a day: allow at least two. (For more tips on Disneyland, see pp.14 and 16.)

Main Street

Situated at the park entrance, Main Street takes you back to turn-of-the-century small-town America, to a world of ragtime and barber-shop musicians, old-fashioned gaslights, horse-pulled trolleys, double-decker buses and antique fire engines. Here, brick and wooden-fronted shops with colourful signs (many names on the upstairs windows actually honour Disney employees) try to lure you in with their merchandise.

Attractions in Main Street warrant a look only if you have time at the end of your visit. A cinema features old black-and-white Disney films (*Steamboat Willie*, in which Mickey Mouse debuted in 1928, is always showing); a penny arcade presents self-winding picture-card stories; and **The Walt Disney Story** introduces you to the man himself and his early cartoons, and reveals some of the secrets behind *Audio-Animatronics* (special, patented lifelike characters activated by a system of pneumatic and hydraulic transmission).

13

THEME PARK NUTS AND BOLTS

All the parks are free to children under three years of age and offer reductions for senior citizens and annual passes. Phone in advance for exact opening hours. Summer months run from Memorial Day (last Monday in May) or mid-June to Labor Day (1st Monday in September).

When to Visit. Outside the school holidays and the months of June to September, lines are much shorter or non-existent, but the parks have shortened opening hours and some rides are not operating.

Avoiding the Lines. Get to the parks early. Do the most popular rides straightaway, and also at meal, show and parade times. Avoid Saturdays; Sundays and weekdays are more peaceful.

Height Restrictions. For Disneyland, Knott's and Magic Mountain, you need to be over a certain height to go on many of the most exhilarating rides.

The Re-Entry System. You can leave the confines of any park and return later that day by getting your hand stamped on the way out.

Money-Saving Tips. Eat the main meal of the day and buy all necessities – camera film, etc – *outside* the park. If your hotel operates a free shuttle to the park, take it: you won't have to pay for car parking. Look for park discounts in brochures in the hotel foyer.

Disneyland, 1313 Harbor Boulevard, Anaheim, CA 92803-3232; tel. (714) 999-4565. *Directions*: 27 miles (43km) southeast of central Los Angeles (take the Harbor Boulevard exit off I5). *Passes*: one day $30, $24 children 3-11; two days $55, $44 3-11s; three days $75, $60 3-11s . *Parking*: $6. *Opening hours*: summer, daily 8am-midnight; rest of year, weekdays 10am-6pm, Sat 9am-midnight, Sun 9am-10pm or midnight; times vary for Christmas and Easter holidays.

Knott's Berry Farm, 8039 Beach Boulevard, Buena Park, CA 90620; tel. (714) 827-1776; tel. (714) 220-5200 for recorded information on opening hours. *Directions*: 6 miles (10km) northwest of Disneyland; 20 miles (32km) southeast of L.A. (exit south on Beach Boulevard off I5). *Passes*: $25.95, $15.95 children 3-11. Admission for all after 6pm is $12.95. *Parking*: $5. *Opening hours*: summer, Sun-Thurs 9am-11pm, Fri and Sat 9am-midnight;

rest of year, weekdays 10am-6pm, Sat 10am-10pm, Sun 10am-7pm.

San Diego Wild Animal Park, 15500 San Pasqual Valley Road, Escondido, CA 92027-9614; tel. (619) 480-0100/(619) 747-8702. *Directions*: 30 miles (48km) north of downtown San Diego via Highway 163/I15 (take the Via Rancho Parkway exit). *Passes*: $17.45, $10.45 children 3-11. *Parking*: $3. *Opening hours*: summer, Thurs-Sun 9am-10pm, Mon-Wed 9am-7pm; rest of year 9am-5pm.

San Diego Zoo, 2920 Zoo Drive, Balboa Park, San Diego, CA 92103; tel. (619) 234-3153. *Directions*: north of downtown San Diego in Balboa Park (follow signs from Freeway 163). *Passes*: $13 adults, $6 children 3-11 (bus tour $3 adults, $2.50 children 3-11). *Parking*: free. *Opening hours*: daily 9am-5/6pm. Joint pass for Zoo and Wild Animal Park (if visited within 5 days) $24, $13 children 3-11.

Sea World, 1720 South Shores Road, San Diego, CA 92109; tel. (619) 226-3815; tel. (619) 226-3901 for recorded information on opening hours. *Directions*: on Mission Bay, 10 minutes' drive north of downtown San Diego (take Sea World Drive exit west off I5). *Passes*: $27.95, $19.95 children 3-11. *Parking*: $5. *Opening hours*: summer, Sun-Thurs 9am-10pm, Fri and Sat 9am-11pm; rest of year 10am-5/6pm.

Six Flags Magic Mountain, 26101 Magic Mountain Parkway, Valencia, CA 91355; tel. (805) 255-4111. *Directions*: 30 minutes north of Hollywood (take Magic Mountain Parkway exit off I5). *Passes*: $28, $15 children under 48in (1.20m). *Parking*: $5. *Opening hours*: summer, Sun-Thurs 10am-10pm, Fri and Sat 10am-midnight; end of March to mid-June and two weeks around Christmas daily 10am-6/8/10pm; rest of year weekends only, 10am-6/8/10pm.

Universal Studios, 100 Universal City Plaza, Universal City, CA 91608; tel (818) 508-9600. *Directions*: north of central Hollywood in the San Fernando Valley (take either the Universal Center or Lankershim Boulevard exits off Hollywood Freeway 101). *Passes*: $29.95, $23.95 children 3-11. Two-day tickets: $50.50, $40 3-11s. *Parking*: $5. *Opening hours*: summer, daily 7am-11pm; rest of year 9am-7pm.

If the park is a big wheel, Central Plaza, at the end of Main Street, acts as its hub, with each of the seven lands on a spoke. We have covered the lands in a clockwise order.

Adventureland

One of Disneyland's original themed areas – with bamboo huts, lush vegetation and live steel-drum music – has altered little since the early years. The arrival in the spring of 1995 of the new **Indiana Jones** attraction will change this (and doubtless be the park's most popular ride for some time). You'll be invited on a transport-jeep expedition through the ruins of an ancient temple, searching for Indy.

At present, the main component of Adventureland is the **Jungle Cruise** – a jokey, 10-

---

Tips for Disneyland

Length of Visit. Two days is the minimum time to spend in the park if you want to go on most of the rides.

Avoiding the Lines. Waiting times are indicated outside each attraction, but lines can be deceptively long – sometimes hidden inside the attraction. Fantasyland rides move slowly; Splash Mountain, Star Tours and the newest rides – at present Roger Rabbit's Cartoon Spin – have the longest lines (up to an hour-and-a-half in summer). Do these first thing in the morning or during a parade.

Early Starts. Main Street opens half an hour early. In peak season, hundreds of visitors rush from here to the big rides. Occasionally, two-day Funrise Passports are available from hotels, letting you into Toontown an hour early on one day only.

Dining and Shopping. For dining, consider popping over to the Disneyland Hotel on the Monorail. For shopping, Main Street stays open for half an hour after the official closing time, but is less busy mid-afternoon.

minute riverboat tour into a tropical forest. The *Audio-Animatronics* wildlife you see on the way, ranging from hippos to headhunters, is at times amazingly lifelike. Many images originated from the film *The African Queen*.

In what could claim to be the park's oddest show, the **Enchanted Tiki Room** hosts a 225-strong singing and whistling animated bird choir. At the top of the 70ft (20m) high, banyan-like Disneydendron, **The Swiss Family Treehouse** (inspired by the popular *The Swiss Family Robinson* story) is worth a climb only if the line is short.

*S*weet respite – sunglasses and ice-cream are fitting extras all year round at Disneyland.

New Orleans Square

New Orleans Square is one of the prettiest areas of the park. Seductive boutiques lurk behind delicate wrought-iron and shuttered façades, while a blues or Dixieland band plays in front of terraced cafés overlooking a rigged sailing ship and a tiered sternwheeler. It's also got two highly imaginative attractions.

The scale and detail of **Pirates of the Caribbean** are astonishing. Your boat meanders through a Louisiana swamp, descends rapids and finally gets caught up in a full-scale sea battle, with a pirate ship firing broadsides on to a fort. As you witness the drunken pirates ransacking the port and getting down to some serious womanizing, look closely at

17

individual faces and gestures: this is Disney animation at its most impressive.

Haunted Mansion isn't all that frightening, but it's definitely entertaining. The walls, doors and paintings in the waiting room suddenly elongate before you're whisked off in black buggies on a superbly conceived journey, where hologram figures unexpectedly pop up in the main hall and ghosts jump out from behind tombstones to perform a song-and-dance routine. Expect the shock of your life as you exit.

Critter Country

This cool corner of the park is backwoods country of tall pines, elms and timber ranches, where the twangs of the banjo and fiddle can often be heard. **Splash Mountain** is the big draw here. As you can watch the log boats whoosh down the 45-degree, 52ft (15m) long, 40mph (65kph) drop and hear the screams from far away, you know what to expect. The 10-minute teaser of a journey inside the mountain

introduces animated characters such as Brer Rabbit, Brer Bear and Brer Fox, from the 1948 movie *Song of the South*. If you weren't spending the whole ride worrying about the final drop, it would be a lot of fun. Expect a wait.

You can usually get in quickly to see the 15-minute show in the **Country Bear Playhouse**. A bevvy of lovable, funny animated bears sing catchy tunes, along with the moose, buffalo

Meet the Gang

Mickey Mouse himself is Disneyland's biggest attraction. Over 50 adult-sized versions of the mouse and his gang (Minnie, Donald and co.) appear in the park at any one time: look for them in Town Square, at Sleeping Beauty Castle and in Toontown. It's fun to see how even the most grumpy grown-up is soon won over by their enchanting gestures. Although they can't speak, the gang can write: buy an autograph book for them to sign.

and deer heads on the wall. The Christmas show is definitely the best; the rest of the year the troupe performs a summer vacation show.

Frontierland

Frontierland, the land of the Wild West, bristles with cacti. Here, Western stores like Bonanza Outfitters and a shooting arcade tempt you in, and the sounds of a steam engine, steamboat whistle and country music fill the air. The **Golden Horseshoe Jamboree**, a slick, lively show with can-can girls and dancing cowboys performs regularly in the saloon (book your tickets at the reservations office on Town Square).

Big Thunder Mountain Railroad gets top billing here. The roller-coaster ride on a runaway train round the precariously piled landmark rock is classic Disney, with the scare factor low but the entertainment one high. The rattling journey takes you through a realistic gold-rush setting in the good ol' Southwest, down into beautiful caves, then into

canyons harbouring packs of coyotes, and finally narrowly escapes falling rocks and rushing waterfalls.

The leisurely cruise on the **Mark Twain Steamboat**, a beautiful and romantic 5/8th-scale reconstruction of a Mississippi original, plies the Rivers of America. Look out for a settler's cabin afire, an Indian camp and a grizzly bear on the banks. **Tom Sawyer Island**, in the middle of Rivers

*B*rave adventurers and daredevils will find plenty to keep them occupied in Disneyland. **19**

of America, is reached by a raft. Its treehouse, rope-suspension bridge, rocks to climb and caves to explore make a dream playground – perfect for kids if they've been standing in line for a while. Don't let them miss Fort Wilderness at the far end, a wonderfully authentic stockade.

Fantasyland

Disneyland is, arguably, Fantasyland. Here, the best-known fairytales are brought to life in charming, animated rides and fairground attractions, such as **Dumbo the Flying Elephant** (can there be anything more adorable than a flock of flying dumbos?). The land boasts the park's biggest concentration of attractions in a compact space, so can be very crowded.

Entering from Central Plaza, you pass under the arch of **Sleeping Beauty Castle**, its spindly pink towers and blue-and-gold roofs the very symbol of Disneyland. (A forced perspective makes it look bigger than it actually is.) At the back of the castle, a courtyard framed by gingerbread buildings contains five gentle rides, each just a couple of minutes long, telling a story based on their namesake fairytale. As ever, detail in the animation is quite extraordinary.

Choose one or two to which your party knows the story: **Pinocchio's Daring Journey**, for example, can be rather confusing otherwise.

Snow White's Scary Adventures follows the young girl into the forest with the wicked witch. On **Mr Toad's Wild Ride** you get into madcap adventures driving around London and the English countryside. **Peter Pan's Flight** is a firm favourite, not least because you get to 'fly' in Jolly Roger sailing ships to Never Land. For **Alice in Wonderland**, you follow Alice down the rabbit hole on a caterpillar to meet the Queen of Hearts and the Cheshire Cat, among many others.

For ingenuity, if not sheer charm, the *Audio-Animatronics* of these rides overshadow **Storybook Land Canal Boats**, which make a circuit round fairytale places of miniature crenellated castles, adorable villages and pretty windmills. It's hard to believe the in-scale plants and trees are all alive. The **Casey Jr Circus Train** follows the same course.

It's a Small World encapsulates the charm and innocence of Disneyland. The boat journey through a happy world of smiling and singing puppet choirs, animals and flora might entrance young kids.

The white cement and steel pyramid of the Matterhorn, an impressive 1/100th-scale reproduction of the Swiss original, towers above all else in the theme park. Cable cars run through it on the way to Tomorrowland, but to experience the mountain properly you need to take the jerky, white-knuckle ride of **Matterhorn Bobsleds**. It's one of Disneyland's less sophisticated attractions, but fun nevertheless.

Parades and Shows

Check the leaflet you're given as you enter the park for times of events, and secure a prime watching spot early. The **Lion King Parade** (daily during holiday periods, weekends otherwise), based on Disney's film *The Lion King*, made its debut in summer 1994. The sensational **Fantasmic** (nightly during holiday periods, weekends otherwise) lays on a concoction of pyrotechnics, laser lights and cinematic images projected on to mist screens, and involves Disney characters on board barges and the steamboat, plus acrobatic pirates on the rigging of the sailing ship.

In the old-time favourite, **Main Street Electrical Parade** (nightly in summer, some weekends otherwise), Disney characters waltz by on floats lit up by hundreds of fairy lights. The fireworks display, **Fantasy in the Sky**, happens only in summer, starting between 9 and 9.30pm. **The Very Merry Christmas Parade** (Thanksgiving to New Year's Week) involves Santa and hundreds of performers and musicians.

On your way round, watch out for the abominable snowman.

 Toontown

Everything in the land of the toons is either squidgy, rubbery, screwy, loony or plain crazy: houses bulge, manholes talk, fountains honk and props boxes hoot. The 3-D cartoon environment's sheer perfection – in which a downtown, suburbs and rural areas are seamlessly held together in a totally mad fashion – outshines any other part of the park.

The toons (cartoon characters) have lived here for many years, so the story goes, but only opened their hideaway to visitors in 1993.

At the residential end of Toontown is **Mickey's House**, through which you wander at your own pace, admiring the Mouseway piano and books in the sitting-room (*Cheese and Peace, The Old Mouse and the Sea*). Out at the back, meet the mouse himself in his movie studio barn and tell him what you think of his little home. **Minnie's House**, next door, is all pink and purple. It's more feminine, of course, and covered in hearts and notes from Mickey. Don't miss the crazy dishwasher and fridge stuffed with cheese-chip ice-cream. In the inflatable **Goofy's Bounce House**, kids can throw themselves against the furniture with abandon. **Gadget's Go Coaster**, a mini roller-coaster made of oversized toys, does a few loops in its short trip and is good for younger kids (over three), but expect a wait.

Take the wobbly **Jolly Trolley**, seemingly run by clockwork, to downtown and its batty town hall, school, bank and post office. At the garage, you're advised to 'Honk for service', and a road sign warns of 'Gags ahead'. Everything reveals some mad surprise.

At The Cab Co., take the park's latest ride, **Roger Rabbit's Cartoon Spin**. Along the back alleys of Toontown, Jessica Rabbit, Baby Herman and other toons pop out to meet you. The ride itself is a surreal rendering of the Fantasyland rides, but here your cab spins through cartoon gag situations.

Tomorrowland

Stark Tomorrowland lacks the charm of the other worlds and feels dated in parts, but here

you'll find the greatest concentration of thrill rides and shows. It's also the embarkation point for the **Monorail**, whose trip to the Disneyland Hotel and back provides good park views. The nonstop silent cars of the **PeopleMover** on its grand tour of Tomorrowland gives a brief introduction to some rides.

The virtual reality of **Star Tours** is a mind-blowing experience. It's the most exciting ride in the park, with none of the sheer fear that is the usual hallmark of a roller-coaster. R2D2 and CP3O chat while you wait in line, then flight attendants usher you into a flight simulator-cum-space ship. You watch your space ship take you on an out-of-control voyage based on the movie *Star Wars*, while the cabin shudders, rocks and jolts in time with the action. It really feels as if those missiles and meteors just missed!

Space Mountain, by contrast, is Disney's gut-wrenching, roller-coaster experience. Before embarkation, you gather in a space port cloaked in a **23**

green penumbra and surrounded by flashing lights and metallic voices. Step into the carriages, or rockets, for a breathtaking journey through space. You're travelling at 30mph (50kph), but the virtual pitch-black conditions make it feel much faster. If you can bear to keep your eyes open, the galactic vision of twinkling stars is very beautiful.

On **Submarine Voyage**, it seems the vessel submerges when in fact it does nothing of the sort. Peering through portholes on an underwater world as you journey round the lake, you encounter a giant squid and some mermaids, and discover the lost city of Atlantis. The ride is corny, but fun.

Tomorrowland's two short 20-minute films offer state-of-the-art cinematic techniques, shown in large auditoria. Waiting time is usually minimal. **Circle-Vision** shows amazing geographical sequences in *Wonders of China* and *American Journeys*, on a 360-degree screen that envelops the whole theatre (*American Journeys* is the more exhilarating of the two). In the Magic Eye Theater, you watch through 3-D glasses as **Captain EO**, alias Michael Jackson, overcomes the forces of evil through his music and dancing, turning ghoulish monsters into dancing, fun-loving prototypes.

Disneyland Hotel

Stay in the Disneyland Hotel and you'll be waking to the strains of 'When you wish upon a star'. On the hotel's marina, you can take pedalo rides, operate model boats, and watch choreographed water shows. With a 50s-style diner, steak house, seafood, Italian and buffet restaurant, dining options are excellent – and you can drink alcohol. Furthermore, Disney characters make impromptu visits. For nightlife, try the civilized wine bar and Country and Western bar. If the park has shut before you have finished shopping for souvenirs, make use of the hotel's many shops.

KNOTT'S BERRY FARM

Regulars among Knott's 5 million annual visitors admit to a sense of emotional attachment to the park. Knott's has come a long way since its Ghost Town origins in 1940 (see p.10), to include thrill rides, big song-and-dance shows, educational exhibits and, more recently, the adorable Snoopy.

Attractions generally lack the finesse and attention to detail that would elevate them to Disney status, while the live shows are uneven, but the park's charm lies in its home-spun feel.

Ghost Town, the most atmospheric of the six themed areas, covers a good third of Knott's Berry Farm. Teeny tots will want to head straight for Camp Snoopy, however, while older children, teenagers and other intrepids march off towards the roller-coasters and fairground rides of the Roaring '20s and Fiesta Village.

Camp Snoopy

Kids demand cuddles from big, white, furry Snoopy as he greets them at the camp entrance. Pine trees and streams provide the camp feel, reinforced by the khaki, scout-like uniforms worn by the staff.

Snoopy the ace pilot's flying scarf provides the benchmark

*W*ho can resist a hug from the world's largest and most adorable beagle?

25

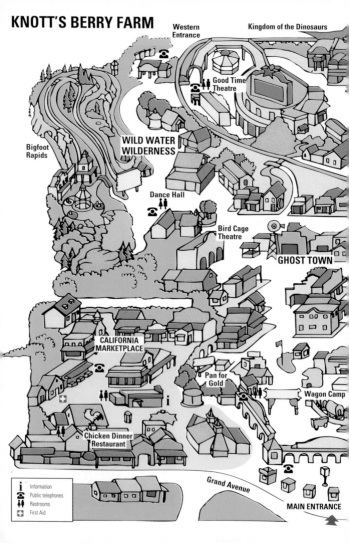

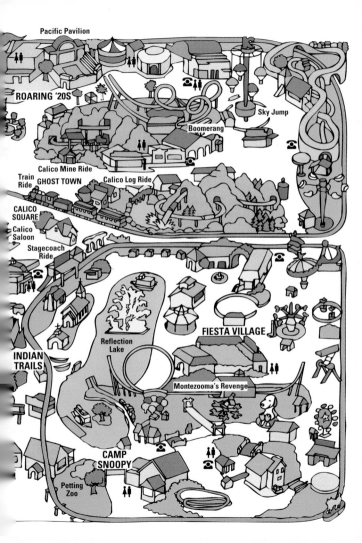

for height on most of the short, scaled-down rides. Some of the most popular ones include the yellow **Camp Bus** which takes you round and round in the air; **Timberline Twister**, a miniature roller-coaster; **Beary Tales**, a house full of bears at work and play; and **Red Baron**, where kids get to fly picturesque World War I planes with Snoopy looking on from his dog house.

You can also pop into the **Petting Zoo** to see Herbie, a giant tortoise born in 1923, and hang around for **Snoopy's Animal Friends'** show, featuring a performing pig, rabbit and cat. For budding scientists, **Thomas Edison's Inventor's Workshop** explains how electricity and magnets work.

Ghost Town

The weathered, arcaded and balconied buildings of Ghost Town, which include a funeral home, church, schoolhouse, laundry, barbershop, saloon and blacksmiths, are not faithful replicas, but well and truly authentic pieces, culled by Mr Knott himself from the Wild West over the years (see p.9).

The 'locals' in Ghost Town go about their daily business:

Tips for Knott's Berry Farm

Length of Visit. One full day is just right.

Avoiding the Lines. The park never gets as crowded as Disneyland, but in summer the big-thrill rides can have hour-long waits: do them first thing in the morning or last thing before closing time. Out of season, waits for rides are rarely more than five minutes long.

When to Visit. There are no lines out of season, but the park loses some of its atmosphere as many shows aren't running.

Dining and Shopping. Hit the California Marketplace next door to the park. It opens and closes before and after the park.

the smithy mends horseshoes, the schoolmistress tidies her classroom, and booted and braced cowboys slouch around menacingly (try to catch an impromptu shoot-out). Sad Eye Joe the horse thief sits in the one-man jail (if you chat with him, you may be in for a big surprise).

Many stores sell fascinating items. The Geode Shop has fossils and precious stones, the gun shop silver bullets and the knife shop lethal weapons such as the Arkansas Toothpick. In the Print Shop Bulletin, have your name put on a wanted poster; in the Pitchur Gallery

*Y*ou can pose with the resident blacksmith or take the stagecoach ride in Ghost Town.

have your photo taken in 19th-century finery.

At **Pan for Gold**, for a couple of dollars you can try to get rich quick. Shake the pan just below the surface of the water, keeping the heavier specks of gold in while sieving the sand out: whatever gold's left you keep as a great souvenir. Look in on **Western Trails Museum**, crammed full with everything from flint lock rifles to barbed wire and a model of the Vienna Ferris Wheel. There's usually a bit of a wait for the classic **stagecoach** ride, on which four white horses pull an original coach on a six-minute journey round the park. Meanwhile, rides in the antique carriages pulled by the full-size chugging and hissing 19th-century **steam train** can be disturbed by hold-ups.

There's nothing at all spooky about the **Haunted Shack**. The series of radically sloping rooms make for fun optical illusions. On the little ore-carrying wagons of the **Calico Mine Ride**, you enter a mountain to see animated characters beavering away in a big chamber.

Next door, on the popular **Calico Log Ride**, you sit in hewn-out logs as they flow through another mountain, which is inhabited by wild animals – be prepared for a radical drop at the end of the journey.

As far as shows are concerned, the **Bird Cage Theatre** provides melodramas in old-fashioned music-hall style, complete with a hissing and cheering audience. The lovely **Calico Saloon** lays on high-kicking gals in ra-ra skirts. It's fun to sit up in old wagons to watch **Knott's Wild West Stunt Show**, but the show itself is disappointing, with more slapstick than acrobatics.

Indian Trails

This small Indian settlement, with colourful totem poles and wigwams painted with buffalo and horses, is really an off-shoot of Ghost Town. Chat to Indian craftspeople as they make canoes and fashion original necklaces, or watch the Native American dances that take place on a stage surrounded by Navajo stone huts.

Wild Water Wilderness

The big draw here is **Bigfoot Rapids**, a scare-free ride for all the family – if no one minds getting wet. Large rubber rafts are buffeted, spun and splashed as they descend the white-water course. In the **Wilderness Nature Center** nearby, you learn about Californian Bigfoot sightings.

Roaring '20s

This 1920s fairground scene, constantly swinging to the sounds of jazz, comes alive at night in glowing neon. Like any fair, it's at its best when busy – when the many arcades are rattling away, winners are carting around outsize cuddly toys, and the Good Time Theatre is hosting Broadway-style song-and-dance shows.

Rides range from the traditional bumper cars to high-tech **XK-1**, in which you can rotate your rocket through 360 degrees. Doubtless, you'll have sized up **Boomerang**, the sea-blue roller-coaster with those sick-making loops. Cars are

Sky Jump's 20-storey high, stomach-churning parachute drop always delivers a happy landing at Knott's Roaring '20s.

cranked up and up and up, then freefall through three loops that twist and turn you upside down, before doing the whole thing again – backwards. It feels as frightening as it looks.

Sky Jump is not for the faint-hearted. You're lifted up

Montezooma's Revenge's loop is quite an experience – but is best avoided after lunch.

20 storeys in a cage, with only a grille beneath your feet. Your stomach does a turn at the start of the descent, but then it's plain sailing (or parachuting), as colourful cloths billow as you drop to the ground.

The animated **Kingdom of the Dinosaurs** ride appeals to all. Professor Wells' time machine gets it wrong, whisking you back to the time of cavemen and mammoths, and then a further 200 million years to a

growling, roaring, generally frightening *Tyrannosaurus rex*. In the Dinosaur Center, a palaeontologist with a range of fossils and wall charts answers your questions.

Roaring '20s puts on a couple of good shows. The cosy **Pacific Pavilion** allows you to get right up close to the performing sea lions and dolphins. **Cloud 9**, meanwhile, features the excellent 30-minute *Sea Dream* fantasy 3-D movie.

Fiesta Village

In Mexican Fiesta Village you will find a host of markets, terracotta-tiled fountains, flamen-co dancers, mariachi players and cantinas – naturally the best place in the park for Mexican food.

Fiesta Village's half-dozen colourful fairground attractions range from **Tampico Tumbler**, which spins you in every direction, to **Merry-Go-Round**, an antique carousel populated by zoo animals.

Overshadowing all the others, stands the yellow beast of **Montezooma's Revenge**. Its 31-second ride catapults you from 0 to 55mph (0-90kpm) in under 5 seconds through a giant loop, leaving you aching and shaky, but totally exhilarated from the experience.

Festivals and Shows

For 12 nights during **Halloween Haunt**, the biggest Halloween show in the world, Knott's becomes a spooky place. The special event is great for teenagers, but may scare small children. (You can get tickets in advance from Ticketmaster or at the park gates.) From Thanksgiving to Christmas, **Knott's Berry Farm Christmas Crafts Festival** transforms Ghost Town into an 1880s Victorian shopping village. In the two weeks over Easter, the **Country Fair** hosts pie-eating and cow-milking contests. Fireworks displays are staged every night in peak season.

Anaheim and Vicinity

Outside its two famous theme parks, Disneyland and Knott's Berry Farm, Anaheim and vicinity have little visual appeal, but offer a range of attractions for all the family.

Just down the road from Knott's Berry in Buena Park, the **Movieland Wax Museum** has over 250 life-size wax replicas of movie and TV stars

---

ORANGE COUNTY HIGHLIGHTS

Mission San Juan Capistrano, *Camino Capistrano and Ortega Highway; tel. (714) 248-2049.* Open 8.30am-5pm. $4, $3 children 3-11. Beautiful old Californian Mission. (See p.36)

Movieland Wax Museum, *7711 Beach Boulevard, Buena Park; tel. (714) 522-1154.* Open summer 9am-10.30pm, winter 10am-9.30pm. $12.95, $6.95 children 4-11. Combination ticket with Ripley's $16.90, $9.75 children 4-11. (See above)

Queen Mary Seaport, *1126 Queens Highway, Long Beach; tel. (310) 435-3511.* Open 10am-6pm (in summer until 9pm Fri and Sat). Free. Tours $5, $3 children 4-11. Luxurious ocean liner converted into a floating hotel and museum. (See p.39)

Raging Waters, *111 Raging Waters Drive, San Dimas; tel. (909) 592-6453.* Open April, May, Sept, Oct weekends 10am-6pm, June-Sept up to 10pm. $20, $12 children, free for children under 42in (1.05m). Big-thrill water rides. (See p.36)

Ripley's Believe It or Not!, *7850 Beach Boulevard, Buena Park; tel. (714) 522-7045.* Open summer 9am-10.30pm, winter 10am-9.30pm. $8.95, $5.25 children 4-11. (See opposite)

Wild Rivers, *8770 Irvine Center Drive, Irvine; tel. (714) 768-WILD.* Open May and Sept weekends 11am-5pm, June 11am-5pm, July and Aug 10am-8pm. $16.95, $12.95 children 3-9. Water rides for all the family. (See p.36)

across the decades. In varying degrees of verisimilitude, they are portrayed in their most famous roles: Marilyn Monroe in *Gentlemen Prefer Blondes*, Elizabeth Taylor as Cleopatra, Redford and Newman in *Butch Cassidy and the Sundance Kid*. Whole scenes are re-created, from the control room of the Star Ship Enterprise to an upside down set from *The Poseidon Adventure*. The selection of stars is admirably up to date, so bring your camera and find out what it's like to be a paparazzo.

The entrance fee to the Wax Museum is steep, but a better-value joint ticket includes a visit to **Ripley's Believe It or Not!**, across the road. One of a chain of museums devoted to the bizarre, it houses real and simulated objects, and video footage of all sorts of tall stories, including 'The man who ate cigarettes', and many odd and fascinating facts about Hollywood and earthquakes.

The **Crystal Cathedral**, situated southeast of Disneyland at 12141 Lewis Street, Garden Grove, is no ordinary house of

The shimmering glass tower of the Crystal Cathedral harbours a no less amazing interior.

worship. Outside, some 10,000 panes of mirror glass cover the whole building. Inside, the ceiling of the vast auditorium is filled with the blue of the sky – a structure built in synthesis with the sunny climate. It's a fitting home for the outspoken evangelist preacher, the Reverend Robert Schuller. **35**

Coastal Orange County

Inland Orange County has little to recommend it scenically, by sharp contrast with the affluent, distinctive beach communities on the coast, dubbed the American Riviera. Vast, sandy beaches and the Pacific Ocean stretch before you – a surfing paradise – and each beach community has its own intriguing atmosphere.

Driving south down the San Diego Freeway, you soon come to the **Mission San Juan Capistrano**. This serene antidote to theme park mayhem is the seventh in the chain of California missions, founded in 1776 by Father Junípero Serra.

The Serra Chapel, the oldest church in the state, has a painted wooden ceiling and a two-tier altarpiece which is covered in dazzling gold-leaf and angelic faces. It stands on the edge of a gorgeous courtyard along with other pantiled lay buildings – work rooms, living quarters – that show artefacts

Wet'n'Wise

For a more controlled environment than a Californian beach, consider a day at one of the two big waterparks not far from Disneyland. There, the waves are as big or as gentle as you like, cafés and restaurants are on hand for a drink or bite to eat, and you can relax on tropical, sandy beaches. Both parks also offer a variety of big-thrill water experiences – vertical drops, white-water rides on inner tubes, and 'dark' rides where you shoot through a black tube. Height limits are set on some of the big rides, but mini-rides are plentiful. **Raging Waters**, 25 minutes north of Anaheim, 30 minutes east of L.A. (where the 10, 210 and 57 freeways meet), also lays on jet-ski stunt shows.

At the African-themed **Wild Rivers**, half an hour southeast of Anaheim just off I-5, you could spend all day lounging in giant-sized jacuzzi pools.

The beautiful Mission San Juan Capistrano stands as a proud reminder of California's past.

from, and re-creations of, the mission's fascinating past.

Some 10 miles (16km) north along Pacific Coast Highway (PCH) lies one-of-a-kind **Laguna Beach**. Away from the roar of traffic along the main road, it's very romantic (some call it California's honeymoon capital), with a chain of coves overlooked by some ideally situated hotels and restaurants. A very eclectic bunch hangs out in Laguna, where in the same street a Rolls Royce is parked next to a battered VW van, a coffee house touts lentil soup, and a bookshop-cum-café hosts regular astrological and psychic sessions.

Since early this century, Laguna has harboured an artists' **37** colony, hence the many modern art galleries along PCH. Its summer Festival of the Arts is best known for the *Pageant of the Masters* – stunning nightly re-creations of paintings and statuary using live models.

Twenty minutes north of Laguna, the far larger conurbation of **Newport Beach** is a long-established family resort for the well-to-do. Skip the inland development and follow the yacht- and island-dotted harbour round to Balboa Peninsula. On one side of the slinky strip of land lies a fabulous big beach with two piers. At the base of Newport Pier, hungry gulls perch on the few protected shacks of the small-time Dory Fishing Fleet. On the harbour side opposite Balboa Pier stands The Pavilion, once a Victorian bathhouse, now the focal point for a pretty little amusement park, harbour and whale-watch cruises. It is also the departure point for a three-car ferry across to quaint Balboa Island.

The endless sands of **Huntington Beach**, some 10 miles (16km) to the north of Newport Beach, are one of the world's surfing meccas. Even on a cloudy winter's day, hundreds of surfers turn out to ride the waves. It makes a great specta-

*T*he rides are as hair-raising or as gentle as you wish at the Raging Waters park.

cle from the downtown pier, and it's fun to wander through the many shops dedicated to the latest surf paraphernalia.

In June, the resort hosts the world's largest surfing contest. On summer evenings, it's always barbecue and party time on the beach.

You can spot the three red-and-black funnels of the largest passenger ship ever built long before you reach her. The **Queen Mary** arrived in the port of industrial Long Beach in 1967, after a long and prestigious career as the most luxurious ocean liner of her time. Today, she's a floating museum and luxury hotel. Spend a night on board if you so wish: you can get an inexpensive standard hotel room (without a porthole) or swan about in one of the panelled Art Deco suites.

The sheer scale of the ship is overwhelming: a walk round the deck runs a good quarter of a mile. A fascinating guided tour takes you to the indoor pool, warehouse-sized boiler-room, the suites and first-class lounge, too. Alternatively, you can enjoy a drink in the Art Deco Observation Bar, shop in the Crown Jewels and dine in style at Sir Winston's.

The dome adjacent to the ship, and similar to a giant golf ball, until recently held Howard Hughes's vast, wooden flying boat, *The Spruce Goose*, intended to carry 750 passengers. Developers have yet to decide with what attraction to fill the space.

The Queen Mary has played host in the past to many of the world's most famous people.

Los Angeles Theme Parks

The entertainment capital of the world boasts a vast number of attractions, but the best family fun to be had is at its theme parks. The city's most famous park, Universal Studios in the San Fernando Valley, is also a massive working movie and TV studio. Here and in some of Los Angeles's many other studios you can gain an insight into how films and TV programmes are made. Some 21 miles (34km) northwest of Universal in Valencia, the amazing

---

Tips for Universal Studios

Length of Visit. In high season (during school holidays and from June to September), allow one very full day to cover the park. With shorter waits out of season, one day is ample time. If you plan your time carefully, using the Entertainment Schedule, you can watch shows consecutively.

Avoiding the Lines. Shows take place in large arenas, but go on the only two low-capacity rides, ET and Back to The Future, early in the day. To avoid long waits for the Studio Tram Ride, you're given a registration time as you enter the park: if you miss the specified time, you can always go later.

When to Visit. The studios lay on a couple of extra shows in summer; otherwise there are no disadvantages for visiting Universal Studios out of season.

Dining and Shopping. Don't overlook Universal CityWalk (see p.44), adjacent to the park.

TV Shows. Go to the Audiences Unlimited booth in the heart of the Entertainment Center for inquiries. (See also p.133.)

New Events. The Flintstone Show, Universal's most expensive ever, was inaugurated simultaneously with the movie in 1994. A Jurassic Park ride is scheduled for 1996.

roller-coaster rides of Six Flags Magic Mountain offer more traditional theme park entertainment. Under the ownership of Time Warner, the park is also developing movie-themed attractions.

UNIVERSAL STUDIOS

As well as being one of the world's most popular theme parks, with 5 million visitors a year, Universal Studios boasts another 'first', as the world's largest motion-picture and biggest TV studio.

The layout of Universal can be confusing. Most of the theme park lies atop a hill in the **Entertainment Center**, which is made up of streets of re-created architecture from all parts of the world, and large arenas for shows either related to well-known Universal productions, or used to demonstrate movie stunts and tricks.

The quarter-of-a-mile long Starway escalator takes you far down the hillside to the much smaller **Studio Center**, where a few sound stages hold other attractions. You'll also

*L*ive film and cartoon characters provide a bubbly welcome to Universal Studios.

get to meet many of the remarkable clones of Laurel and Hardy, Charlie Chaplin, Groucho Marx and Marilyn Monroe, and unlike in other theme parks, these characters will actually talk to you. The real, **41** working part of the studios lies down here too. You can only visit this area on the 45-minute Studio Tram Ride, a part-thrill, part-insight tour of the back-lots, the tour is a little rushed, however, and other studios offer more leisurely, educational visits (see p.46).

Studio Tram Ride

This is a trip round a working studio, so you never know what you might see – maybe a movie star having coffee, or filming of the latest blockbuster, or maybe no action at all. Every tour, however, whisks you round the backlots, where artisans toil away fashioning the latest sets.

You move from New York to the Old West to Mexico, as the guide points out locations for famous movies: the court-house from the *Back to the Future* trilogy, the *Psycho* House, sets from *Spartacus* and *Home Alone 2*. Each and everyone of them is a façade made out of fibreglass and foam.

However, the tour's highlights are the special effects. A bridge collapses and a lake parts as you are crossing them. A flash flood washes away a Mexican village (turn round to see the trees spring back up). The killer-shark Jaws erupts out of a lake, and King Kong – the world's largest animated creature at three storeys tall – assaults the tram as it stands on a tottering Brooklyn Bridge (he gets so close you can smell his banana breath). A two-minute earthquake measuring 8.3 on the Richter Scale causes subway cars to crash, a truck to career out of control and a 60,000-gallon flood.

Studio Center

The ET Adventure is a classic, modern fairytale theme-park ride, which is ideal for young children. You're on a bicycle with ET, accompanying the lovable creature on his journey home. Riding through

Into the jaws of the unknown ... the chase is on with Back to The Future – The Ride.

a forest, evading the headlights of police cars and rising over a twinkling night-time Los Angeles, you finally make it to the Green Planet, where animated flowers and ET lookalikes welcome you. As you leave, catch ET's last words as he bids farewell.

Backdraft the movie was said to have the finest fire effects ever filmed. **Backdraft** the attraction, billed as California's hottest, must come close to equalling them. You experience close up the film's final scene: a warehouse set on fire, with immense flashes of heat, roaring flames and collapsing gantries. Suddenly, it's all going wrong as the platform you're standing on starts

to give way ... Youngsters may find it all a bit too realistic.

In **The World of Cinemagic**, members of the audience help to demonstrate how the DeLorean cars in *Back to the Future* 'fly', how Hitchcock filmed the shower scene in *Psycho* and how sound effects can be produced – sometimes using the most unlikely methods – for a film sequence from *Harry & the Hendersons*.

Entertainment Center

The top three-quarters of the theme park is home to Streets of the World and most of the shops and restaurants. This is where the shows take place, and where you'll find the park's one big-thrill ride, **Back to The Future – The Ride** – not to be missed at any cost. In a lab in the Institute of Future Technology, Doc Brown gives

Universal CityWalk

It's no exaggeration to say that this $100-million, 21st-century mall is at least as stunning as anything in the studios next door. Here, vintage neon fills the pedestrian avenue, lofty palms soar in the steel-latticed central courtyard and a pink 1957 Chevy lies embedded into an ice-cream parlour. A safe haven away from L.A.'s social problems, it presents a utopian retail vision evoking all that's best about the city. Each shop, from the Museum of Neon Art to Think Big (giant golf tees, beer bottles, crayons), Captain Coconuts (stuffed full of toys), Upper Deck (sports gear including basketballs signed by Magic Johnson) and Wizardz (psychic readings upstairs), lays on an incredible display.

The restaurants showcase L.A. dining. There's a pizza café owned by the city's most famous chef, Wolfgang Puck, and a burger joint with a resident DJ. If all this isn't entertainment enough, the cinema complex has no fewer than 18 screens, and in the state-of-the-art arcade, you can be a paparazzo and shoot as many celebrities as possible – with a video camera.

you your pre-flight briefing. Your mission is to catch the delinquent Biff, who's joyriding in a DeLorean sports car. The judders and shakes of the eight-seater time-travelling machine (get in the front if you can) are synchronized with a 3-D film projected on a giant screen that takes you through the courthouse clock, back in time to the ice age, down a volcano, into the jaws of a *Tyrannosaurus rex*, and down a flow of molten lava ... before you finally beat Biff.

Of the four shows, all about 15 minutes long, **Miami Vice** is the most spectacular: speedboats and jet-skis whizz around at full tilt, and swamp buggies, a cargo trawler and even a helicopter get a slice of the action. Expect a surfeit of explosions, flames and shooting.

The **Wild, Wild, Wild West Stunt Show** mixes impressive stunts – three-storey falls and fistfights – with a modicum of slapstick. By the end of the show, the whole set has virtually collapsed. The fun **Animal Actors' Stage** features tricks performed by canine looka-

likes of Lassie and Beethoven, as well as an orang-utan, rat, eagle and pig. The noisy rock show, **Beetlejuice's Graveyard Revue**, mostly appeals to young kids and teenagers.

Making your way from show to show, you'll come across a piece of London – glimpse

Wolfgang Puck's pizza place is one of many colourful restaurants at Universal CityWalk.

Sherlock Holmes smoking a pipe from an upstairs window on Baker Street – and a Parisian street – aren't those the sails of the Moulin Rouge? You can get a room for a dollar in the hotel on Wild West Street, and they're playing pool above the watchmaker's in a New York brownstone. Catch the a cappella Doo Woop Singers performing in a red chevrolet outside Mel's Diner. For a memorable photo, stick your head in the jaws of a 24ft (7m) long shark on Cape Cod Way.

STUDIOS IN ACTION

For a serious snapshot of a real working studio, take the **Warner VIP Tour**, with no special effects or pre-prepared entertainment. Guides take small groups on trolleys round the 110-acre (45ha) lot (the country's second largest), past the offices of Mel Gibson and Clint Eastwood, round the outdoor sets – a jungle made into Sherwood Forest and Tarzan haunts, a Western town, and Gotham City. You get to see

---

Tips for Six Flags Magic Mountain

Length of Visit. You'll be pushed to go on all the roller-coaster and water rides in one day in summer, but should manage it out of season.

Avoiding the Lines. Even out of season, waits for the two- to three-minute roller-coaster rides can be 45 minutes long, increasing to two hours in summer, when the park opens half an hour earlier to allow visitors to get in line. Go on the big rides – particularly Viper, Batman The Ride and Colossus – straightaway, or at lunchtime or last thing in the evening. Water-ride lines are at their longest in the afternoon.

Height Restrictions. For most of the water and roller-coaster rides, you need to be over 48in (1.20m) – 42in (1.05m) for Ninja, and 54in (1.37m) for Viper and Batman.

the most amazing parking lot in the world, where batmobiles are more common than cadillacs. The props shed stocks a 3ft (1m) fly and a Zeppelin.

Usually, you can watch for a few minutes a sitcom being prepared in a sound stage. If you're lucky, the producer and lead actor will come over and have a chat. **Paramount Studios** offers a similar but less elaborate tour.

NBC TV's studio tour of its Burbank headquarters is far less personalized but considerably less expensive. You're whisked round on foot through the carpenters' workshops, the wardrobe department and get demonstrations of how sound effects and visual backdrops are created. You'll probably be able to pop into the studio of **The Tonight Show**, which is the longest-running TV talk show in history. Even better, however, is to try and see it after the tour. Lights flash 'Applause' above your head when you're supposed to clap, and TV screens show what's being transmitted from the four cameras on the studio floor.

They survived it! Six Flags Magic Mountain has some of the most heart-stopping rides.

A commercial break comes up, and immediately the makeup artist rushes on and touches up host Jay Leno's hair, while the prompt whips through the cue boards. A satellite link fails and has to be done again. **47**

(Although the show is 'live on tape', it's filmed at 5pm so that there's a chance for a quick edit before it's sent by satellite around the country.) You can catch the show on TV later that evening – is that you with the booming laugh?

Practical information relating to studio tours and TV shows is listed on p.133.

SIX FLAGS MAGIC MOUNTAIN

Most of Magic Mountain's 3 million annual visitors come seeking heart-pounding excitement – something that this park delivers considerably better than any other in Southern California. With no less than eight riproaring roller-coasters and big-time water rides, the park is perhaps best suited to teenagers and the young at heart. (Strict height restrictions are enforced on the big rides.) Entertainment for small children and the whole family has increased radically in the last decade, with Time Warner at the helm introducing human-sized Bugs Bunny, Daffy Duck and Looney Tunes characters and scaled-down fairground rides. Nonetheless, you may skip the park altogether if you're not looking for big thrills: Disneyland and Knott's Berry Farm's animated attractions have more charm.

Ringed by mountains in the distance, its 260 leafy acres (105ha) far outstrip other California theme parks for sheer size. Ten themed areas circle around and cover a sizeable hill in the middle. If you don't fancy climbing the hill, a Swiss funicular and a monorail take you up, and you can descend the other side by the monorail or a cable car. However, unless you're hurrying around to beat the lines, you should plan your time to minimize walking.

The Roller-Coasters

The thousands of struts that make up the vividly painted coasters (as they're known in the trade) resemble scaffolding erected to build giants' palaces. They look daunting – and they are. The basic premise of a coaster is to take you as high up as possible before dropping you, with the momentum carrying you the rest of the way. In other words, the the pleasure – and the fear – lie partly in the anticipation.

Beginners should start off on Gold Rusher, the least scary of the rides, before moving on to Revolution. Pros should quit pussyfoooting and tackle Viper, Psyclone, Batman and Colossus (and try to get a seat in the front of the cars).

Here's a taste of each ride, working in a clockwise direction from the park entrance.

Flashback, the world's only hairpin drop coaster, takes you through no less than six 180-degree hairpin drops, producing a powerful freefall effect. **Revolution**, with a 360-degree,

The sheer scale of Colossus is a daunting prospect. Hold on to your hats – and cameras.

90ft (27m) high loop, was the world's first giant looping coaster. The ride is surprisingly smooth and relatively gentle. Just looking at **Viper**, the world's tallest and fastest steel coaster, is enough to unnerve you. The beginning of the ride is absolutely terrifying, as you rise to 188ft (57m) before plunging at 70mph (110kph) into massive loops and corkscrews, and being turned upside down seven times.

In **Ninja**, the black trains are suspended from the red track, creating a flying sensation accentuated by the trains swinging from side to side through 180 degrees.

Psyclone, a replica of the 1927 Coney Island Cyclone coaster, is relentlessly thrilling, beginning in a long dark tunnel before erupting into a 95ft (30m) drop, and many more ups and downs and inexplicable doubling-back turns – all to the disturbing sound of creaking wood. Magic Mountain's first coaster, **Gold Rusher**, follows a runaway mine train theme: a scenic journey takes you through lush mountainous landscape. **Freefall** is no coaster but is even more frightening, with an unrestricted 10-storey drop: you're raised up in an elevator cabin and then 'pushed' over the tower's edge into a 2-second, 55mph (90kph) plunge. Waiting for the inevitable to happen is worse than the reality (or is it?).

The smooth and extremely speedy **Batman The Ride**, the park's newest coaster, differs in two important respects: first you go round 360 degrees on the *outside* of the track's loops, and second you sit in floorless ski-lift chairs exposed to the elements with your legs dangling freely, yet miraculously held in position by gravitational forces when you're upside down. The one-of-a-kind 'zero-gravity heartline spin' causes a floating sensation.

By contrast, **Colossus** offers the ultimate traditional ride – the sensible choice for those who like to stay the right way up. The world's largest dual-track wooden roller-coaster (boasting 2 miles or 3km of track) feels a bit bumpier than its high-tech neighbours.

The Water Rides

Stomach-in-the-mouth plunges are the worst (or best) effects in the theme park's water rides. You'll definitely get wet on all of them.

In **Roaring Rapids** (Rapids Camp Crossing), big rubber rafts carry you down a churning, landscaped river. Fate determines who gets the wettest, as water churns over raft and occupants. **Tidal Wave** (Monterey Landing) claims to be Southern California's wettest water flume ride. Large boats descend a 50ft (15m) waterfall, drenching riders and onlookers on the viewing bridge on the splashdown.

Colourful jet-boats go up a hillside through back country in **Jet Stream** (Cyclone Bay), before making a 57ft (17m) plunge into the lake below. For **Log Jammer** (High Sierra Territory), hollow logs float through a narrow channel of moving water before dropping to a wet finish. On **Yosemite Sam Sierra Falls** (High Sierra Territory) – a waterpark-style ride with two-seater rubber rafts twisting and turning through enclosed plastic tubes – you can get soaked.

The Themed Areas

The park divides up into themed areas, but these aren't consistently executed with the detail or panache which you find at other parks.

A sculpted Bugs Bunny on horseback and pretty 1912 carousel are the landmarks of **Six Flags Plaza,** at the entrance of the park. From there, **Baja Ridge** takes you up through a desert setting to **Rapid Camps Crossing** – a Western town from the gold fever days, landscaped with evergreen trees.

You just can't miss **Samurai Summit** on the hill in the centre of the park, as it's topped by the landmark, 486ft (145m) high Sky Tower. Climb it for the view over the park. Picturesque pagodas, Chinese signs and Bhudda statues provide the oriental theme below.

The fairground areas on the northern side of the theme park merge quite indistinguishably at times. **Cyclone Bay** is a **51** beachfront boardwalk based on Coney Island in Brooklyn, with a lifeguard's chair adding to the atmosphere. Set on the edge of a large lagoon, **Monterey Landing**, in the style of a seaside village, offers some old-fashioned entertainment in the form of bumper cars and a blues band. It follows in to the arcades and fairground rides of **Colossus County Fair** and **Pirate's Cove**.

Gargoyles, grey buildings and a replica of the Batmobile create **Gotham City Backlot**, the newest, sprucest area in the park opened in the spring of 1994. Check out the ACME Atom Smasher ride, and Gordon Gearworks, which twirls you into the air as gravitational force pins you to the wall.

Heading back towards the entrance, **High Sierra Territory**, the kiddy-oriented part of the park, is marked by the General Sam Tree, at 140ft (43m) the world's largest man-made walk-through tree, modelled on a giant sequoia. As well as offering a petting zoo and caged coyotes, the rides of **Bugs Bunny World** treat small children to mini versions of a coaster, carousel and so forth. Here, you need to be *under* 54 inches (1.37m) to get to go! This is also where that 'Cwazy Wabit' and his Looney Tunes pals usually hang out.

The Shows

Many shows happen only in summer. Top billing goes to the new stunts and slapstick of the **Police Academy Action Show** in Monterey Landing, and the pyrotechnical extravaganza of the **Batman Stunt Show**, executed to the backdrop of Gotham City, by Mystic Lake. In summer, catch the laser shows and fireworks displays, and any of the following: a musical tribute to classic film greats in **Silver Screen Magic Moments** at Colossus County Fair; the **Cyclone Bay Hypnotist**; a charming Sherwood Forest tale starring Rabbithood in Six Flags Plaza; the Western stunt show of the **High Sierra Gunslingers**, and the hawks, llamas and snakes of **Animals in Action**, in High Sierra Territory.

Los Angeles and Vicinity

L.A. is so vast – the largest urban area in the world – that you need to be very focused on the sights and attractions you wish to see. In this section, we concentrate on Hollywood, Beverly Hills and the main beach resorts. For a more in-depth look at this fascinating city, consult the *Berlitz Pocket Guide to Los Angeles*.

HOLLYWOOD

Around the world, Hollywood means movie studios, film premieres and movie stars, yet today such glamour has become the territory of West Hollywood, Beverly Hills, Burbank and Universal City. Celebrities stay well away from the geographical Hollywood, where only one major working studio, Paramount, remains. The seedy streets of Tinseltown offer just faint echoes of its 1920s and 30s golden era.

Hollywood Boulevard

Far below the 50ft (15m) high letters of the Hollywood sign, erected in 1923 to advertise real estate, Hollywood Boulevard brims with movie memories. However, from La Brea

The largest motion-picture and TV studio in the world offers entertainment on a grand scale.

Avenue down to Vine Street, expect to see a few winos, adult stores and tacky souvenir shops, too.

Along the boulevard from Sycamore Avenue to Gower Street, some 2,000 pink-speckled marble stars lie embedded in the pavement of the **Hollywood Walk of Fame**. Each star pays homage to a celebrity – from Mickey Mouse to Barbra Streisand – and new stars must pay $4,800 for the privilege. Lining each side of the boulevard, gaudy, purple and pink Art Deco buildings, tired-looking movie palaces and murals of movie greats vie for your attention.

The most imposing movie theatre on Hollywood Boulevard, **Mann's Chinese Theatre**, is an attraction in its own right (you must buy a movie ticket to see the ornate interior). Even more fascinating are the 150-odd signatures and handprints that cover the theatre's concrete courtyard. For this eulogy, stars don't need to pay a penny. Some have even left their trademark – George Burns his cigar, Fred Astaire his footprint, Donald Duck his webbed feet ...

Heading east, the **Max Factor Museum** at the corner of Hollywood and Highland has make-up rooms dedicated to beauty treatment in different decades – all customized for blondes, brunettes and redheads. Look out for the Mechanical Osculator (or kissing machine)!

The **Hollywood Wax Museum** is less elaborate than the Movieland Wax Museum (see p.34), but the diverse range of figures – movie stars, singers, presidents (and even a re-creation of Leonardo da Vinci's *Last Supper*) – are entertainingly portrayed.

Further along is the famous **Frederick's of Hollywood**, purveyor of *risqué* lingerie ever since 1947. Its Bra Museum defies the imagination; the collection of undergarments of the famous includes Tony Curtis' bra from *Some Like It Hot*.

Continue along to 1750 North Vine Street to get a look at the 1950s **Capitol Records Building** – shaped like a stack of records with a stylus on top.

WEST HOLLYWOOD

Tucked between Hollywood and Beverly Hills, West Hollywood, a self-governing city since 1984, is home to a large number of restaurants, nightclubs, shops and offices, as well as to a high proportion of artists and a large gay community. It's one of L.A.'s most lively communities,

Even if you don't have an open-top sports car, a drive along Sunset Boulevard is a quintessential L.A. experience. The best part, **Sunset Strip**, runs from Crescent Heights to Doheny Drive. In the evening, huge billboards advertising the latest film and TV releases are lit up, maximizing the effect of their distracting gimmicks. Park your car and take a wander past the city's most famous rock clubs – Whisky A Go Go, The Roxy – as well as the

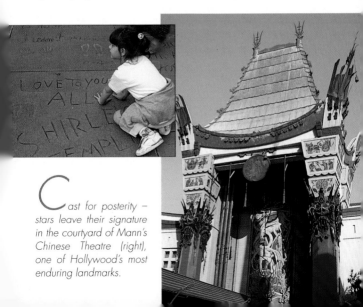

Cast for posterity – stars leave their signature in the courtyard of Mann's Chinese Theatre (right), one of Hollywood's most enduring landmarks.

famous Comedy Store, where many a famous comic started out. Relax at a streetside bistro on Sunset Plaza, and gasp at the lavish Art Deco St James's Club, once an apartment block for movie stars and now an exclusive hotel – as was nearby Château Marmont (see p.68), where Humphrey Bogart proposed to Lauren Bacall and John Belushi died.

On **Melrose Avenue**, at its funkiest between La Brea and Fairfax Avenues, mural art covers shop façades. Wacko, Easy

---

LOS ANGELES HIGHLIGHTS

Frederick's of Hollywood, *6608 Hollywood Boulevard; tel. (213) 466-8506. Open Mon-Sat 10am-6pm, Sun noon-5pm. Free. Lingerie galore, as well as an entertaining Bra Museum. (See p.54)*

George C Page Museum of La Brea Discoveries, *5801 Wilshire Boulevard; tel. (213) 857-6311. Open Tues-Sun 10am-5pm. $5, $2 children 5-10. Fascinating excavations from the nearby tar pits. (See p.57)*

Hollywood Wax Museum, *6767 Hollywood Boulevard; tel. (213) 462-8860. Open Sun-Thurs 10am-midnight; Fri/Sat until 2am. $7.95, $4.95 children 6-12. Wax replicas of the famous. (See p.54)*

Los Angeles Zoo, *5333 Zoo Drive, Griffith Park; tel. (213) 666-4090. Open daily 10am-5pm. Adults $8, $3 children 2-12. Favourite zoo animals are a hit with young children. (See p.60)*

John Paul Getty Museum, *17985 Pacific Coast Highway, Malibu; tel. (310) 458-2003 for parking reservations. Open Tues-Sun 10am-5pm. Free. Beautiful Roman Villa harbouring priceless collections, and created by the eponymous millionaire and art collector. (See p.62)*

Riders, Romp, and others sell records, gay merchandise and youth-oriented gear at the cutting edge of fashion.

Between 40,000 and 10,000 years ago, a couple of miles south in the adjacent Fairfax District, the sticky ponds of the **La Brea Tar Pits** trapped many a mastodon, mammoth and giant sloth. The oily lakes and ponds in front of the museum show life-size replicas of a few mammoths trapped in tar. The **George C Page Museum of La Brea Discoveries** holds the excavated finds.

The museum has a strong educational bent, with meticulous reconstructions of the animals – sometimes fleshed out by fur models. You can even watch grey-haired palaeontologists laboriously cataloguing and cleaning piles of bones with toothbrushes.

A massive, modern complex contains the superb **Los Angeles County Museum of Art** (LACMA), next door. Housed in a five-building structure, the collection covers a vast array of art from around the world, from the primitive to the mod-

*G*lamorous boutiques line Via Rodeo, Los Angeles' most luxurious shopping address.

ern. Highlights include Japanese masterpieces in the Pavilion of Japanese Art; Indian and Asian art and Rodin sculptures in the Ahmanson Building; iconoclastic 20th-century works from Picasso to Warhol in the Anderson Building; and a small number of Impressionist paintings in the Hammer Building. All galleries are open on Friday evening (when piano **57**

and jazz recitals are given on a regular basis) or at weekends; at other times, however, certain galleries are shut.

The **Farmer's Market**, a traditional outdoor collection of eateries and fruit and vegetable stalls, is situated just a few blocks away. It's a great place for lunch. A number of kosher restaurants remain in the area, which was once predominantly Jewish.

BEVERLY HILLS

Hollywood might disappoint, but the reputation of Beverly Hills, a tiny city cocooned within the metropolis of L.A., lives up to its glamorous name.

*L*ucille Ball lived here! Countless other stars choose to make their home in Beverly Hills.

Indeed, some poodles *are* better dressed than the average tourist, and many Rolls Royces *are* parked on innumerable imposing driveways.

The architecturally mundane **Rodeo Drive** is chock-a-block with some of the world's most prestigious clothes and jewellery shops – from Cartier to Christian Dior. Even if you can't afford to shop there, it's free to look. Worth a peek is Rodeo Drive's own small mall, the Rodeo Collection, encased in marble. You can also pop into some of the Drive's more interesting showpieces. Hammacher Schlemmer, at 309, sells gadgets to the super-wealthy; at 273, Fred Hayman has his own bar and displays signed photos of famous visitors (Jackie Collins' reads: 'To Fred – who gives a great store and keeps every Hollywood wife happy'); Adrienne Vittadini, at 319, is where Julia Roberts went on her spending spree in the film *Pretty Woman*. The landmark Regent Beverly Wilshire Hotel, where she and Richard Gere stayed, is a few yards away.

In **residential Beverly Hills** you feel like an intruder in a private estate. On roads lined with picture-postcard pineapple palms, the silence is broken only by the sound of vacuuming and security patrol cars cruising their beat. Such is the variety of house styles, ranging from a French farmhouse to a Tudor manor and Spanish hacienda, that it could be the most elaborate studio backlot ever.

The real estate south of Sunset Boulevard is rarely hidden behind high hedges and is easy to look at. A couple of the most unique homes are the Daliesque house at 507 North Rodeo Drive, and the Witches House at 516 North Walden Drive. To the north of Sunset in the canyons, mansions worth several million dollars are concealed behind high walls and gates. The formal grounds of Greystone, a Tudor manor at 905 Loma Vista, is open to visitors, who can also peer into the empty rooms.

If you want to know who lives or used to live where, try Sunset Boulevard, where vendors hawk maps of the stars' homes. Alternatively, take a **guided minibus tour**. As you sit peering at the mansions, hoping for a big name to step on to their doorstep, it feels like being on safari, trying to spot your quarry in its natural habitat. Many stars live in other homes, so much of the tour tells of famous past residents – 'This is the honeymoon cottage of Marilyn Monroe and Joe DiMaggio', for instance. **59**

GRIFFITH PARK

Griffith Park, spreading across the dramatic Hollywood Hills, is at 4,000 acres (1,620ha) the largest park of any US city. It makes for a whole day's sightseeing, and offers countless activities (see p.104).

From the domed **Observatory**, if the smog is light, you get a panoramic view of L.A., as well as a close look at the Hollywood sign. The Hall of Science inside contains a number of first-rate exhibits, including a Foucault pendulum, demonstrating how the earth rotates on its axis, a scaled-down version of the Hubble Telescope, and a seismograph for registering and recording the strength of earthquakes. There are regular laser shows, and in the evening you can look through a 12in (30cm) telescope at the night sky.

The 115-acre (45ha) **zoo** is worth a visit if all you want is a large stock of traditional zoo animal favourites, and you do not plan to visit the San Diego Zoo or Wild Animal Park (see pp.85 and 88).

The truly imaginative **Gene Autry Western Heritage Museum**, across the parking lot from the zoo, sets out to demythologize the Western story. Bibles, cooking pots and wagons illustrate the lifestyles of the first white pioneers who moved west, while the Spirit of Community section displays original shop signs and saloon items such as cheating devices for poker.

In the Children's Discovery Gallery, kids can put on cowboy gear and pretend to ride a horse. Finally, the Spirit of Imagination section provides an engrossing history of the Western movie genre.

LOS ANGELES BEACHES

It's a short seven miles (11km) from Beverly Hills to the Pacific at Santa Monica. The lovely stretch of coast that runs west

Southern California beaches offer varied pleasures: the golden sands of Santa Monica and (inset) the fun of Venice Beach.

to exclusive Malibu and south to bohemian Veniceis Los Angeles's playground and breathing space.

A beach resort since the 19th century, **Santa Monica** is now a substantial, trendy city with a strong arts base. A pleasant change from car-ridden L.A. is to stroll the vibrant, pedestrian Third Street Promenade, a showcase of Californian shopping and dining whose warehouse bars fill to capacity at the weekend. However, the main reason for visiting awaits below the cliffs – an enormous beach, with every facility imaginable. Above the beach the west coast's oldest pier, dating from 1908, is best known for its Fun Zone fairground, whose antique carousel was operated by Paul Newman in *The Sting*.

On the southern edge of Malibu, west from Santa Monica, stands a dazzlingly beautiful Roman villa, a faithful reproduction of a 1st-century AD Pompeii country residence. The **J Paul Getty Museum** was built by the eponymous oil magnate to house a priceless collection of ancient art which,

along with European decorative art, expands annually thanks to a $1.1 billion endowment. Boldly coloured murals and delicate statuary reveal what the villa's arcades and gardens would have looked like in classical times.

Inside, marble rooms make perfect repositories for classical works – Roman frescos, Greek silverware, Cycladic figures and numerous urns. Upstairs, lush baroque rooms with gilded furniture, embossed wallpaper and Gobelin tapestries complement the period paintings, while other galleries contain a gamut of European painting, from Renaissance triptychs to a fine selection of French Impressionist works including Van Gogh's *Irises*. Although entrance to the museum is free, you *must* reserve your parking space. Phone up to two weeks in advance in summer; there is no on-street parking – tel. (310) 458-2003.

The expansive community of **Malibu** is home to the likes of Barbra Streisand and Jack Nicholson. The stars' beachside compounds and mighty

mansions in the canyons may be strictly private, but don't let that put you off. Come to Malibu for its superb beaches, the best of which are Surfrider, over the pier, and, eight miles (13km) west, Zuma, massive and picturesque. Both are real surfing hotspots.

Named after a doomed, turn-of-the-century project that was intended to re-create the Adriatic port – complete with canals – on the Pacific, **Venice** lies to the south of Santa Monica. It became a hippy mecca in the 60s and still retains the laid-back atmosphere of the flower-power era, particularly on its Ocean Front Walk.

Come on a Sunday afternoon if possible (and stay away after dark). You're unlikely to

*S*an Diego's Mission Bay is a splendid setting for Sea World's carefully thought out park.

have ever seen such a kaleidoscopic spectacle – rap artists on rollerskates, flautists and blues artists, chain-saw jugglers and Indian dancers perform for your pleasure. Stalls offer incense, psychic readings and spray-paint art. Rollerbladers try out high jumps; cyclists ride by, while the punks, rastas, New Age travellers, trendies and family folk all watch on. If that's not enough, check out the real poseurs at Muscle Beach (between 18th and 19th Sts), an outdoor gym. **63**

San Diego Theme Parks

San Diego's theme parks are wildlife parks, with Sea World and San Diego Zoo both within a few minutes' drive of downtown, and Wild Animal Park 30 miles (48km) north of downtown. However, the scale, layout and nature of some of their their attractions – such as shows, monorail and cablecar rides – mean that the parks have much in common with more conventional theme parks in L.A. and Orange County.

Yet here the pleasure for the visitor is more as a spectator than a participator. Sea World's marine shows offer the most family fun, while San Diego Zoo and San Diego Wild Animal Park promote their conservation programmes more actively, lavishing as much, if not more, sensitivity and care on hosts as on guests.

Tips for Sea World

Length of Visit. Allow one full day.

Avoiding the Lines. The park never gets that crowded. In summer, you may have to wait 30 minutes for a few attractions, and should arrive early at the shows to be sure to secure a seat. At other times, you can wander in and out of the attractions and shows freely.

When to Visit. In summer, the park stays open late, puts on a very dramatic waterski show and rounds off the day with fireworks and laser shows over Mission Bay.

Inside Knowledge. Consider taking the 90-minute educational tour of animal care facilities and training centres. Study the times on your 'Meet The Experts' leaflet, which explains when you can drop in on feeding times and talks from carers and trainers at many of the habitats.

A Selection of Hotels and Restaurants in Southern California

Recommended Hotels

In this section, we concentrate on hotels which are convenient for the theme parks. However, in Los Angeles we also suggest places to stay in and around both Hollywood and Beverly Hills, while our San Diego recommendations cover the whole city and its surrounding beaches.

All the establishments listed have a pool, unless otherwise stated. Those in Anaheim, Buena Park, Mission Bay in San Diego, near Universal Studios in L.A., and near Magic Mountain have a free shuttle minibus service to the local theme park.

Price ranges are for a standard double room in high season, excluding breakfast and tax. (Orange County levies a 13% hotel tax and 7.75% sales tax, Los Angeles a 14% hotel tax and 8.25% sales tax, and San Diego a 9% hotel tax and a 7.75% sales tax.) The cost of accommodations drops dramatically out of season, when most hotels as much as halve their rates. Large chain hotels may also offer cut-price accommodations at any time of year, according to how busy they are, while hotels close to the theme parks usually offer good-value special package rates. It's always a good idea to book ahead, especially in the school holidays and summer months.

▐▐▐	Over $150
▐▐	$80-150
▐	Under $80

ANAHEIM

Anaheim Hilton and Towers ▐▐▐

777 Convention Way
Anaheim, CA 92802-3497
Tel. (714) 750-4321
Fax (714) 740-4252
Toll-free 1-800-445-8667
A green glass monolith in Anaheim Convention Center boasting a high number of restaurants and leisure facilities. 1,576 rooms.

Anaheim Marriott ▐▐▐

700 West Convention Way
Anaheim, CA 92802
Tel. (714) 750-8000
Fax (714) 750-9100
Toll-free 1-800-228-9290
An impressive, convention-oriented hotel with good pool areas and

offering both fast-food and haute cuisine. 1,039 rooms.

Anaheim Plaza ▮▮

1700 South Harbor Boulevard
Anaheim, CA 92802
Tel. (714) 772-5900
Fax (714) 772-8386
Toll-free 1-800-228-1357

Long-established and welcoming independent hotel facing Disneyland entrance. Good rooms, some with balconies, in low-rise blocks. Comprehensive facilities. 300 rooms.

Castle Inn ▮

1734 South Harbor Boulevard
Anaheim, CA 92802
Tel. (714) 774-8111
Fax (714) 956-4736
Toll-free 1-800-521-5653

Bizarre, multicoloured motel replete with towers and gargoyles. No public rooms and a tiny pool, but the simple bedrooms are spacious. 200 rooms.

Conestoga Hotel ▮▮

1240 South Walnut Street
Anaheim, CA 92802
Tel. (714) 535-0300
Fax (714) 491-8953
Toll-free 1-800-824-5459

Ranch-style hotel with a Silver Saloon and Chaperral Café; a little gloomy, but original and in a quiet location. 252 rooms.

Disneyland Hotel ▮▮▮

1150 West Cerritos Avenue
Anaheim, CA 92802
Tel. (714) 956-6425
Fax (714) 956-6582

Disney's only Anaheim hotel. The most fun place to stay for Disneyland – and the most convenient, as it's on the monorail. Impeccable facilities and great dining options. A somewhat expensive choice, but regular package deals are on offer. 1,131 rooms.

Howard Johnson Hotel ▮

1380 South Harbor Boulevard
Anaheim, CA 92802
Tel. (714) 776-6120
Fax (714) 33-3578
Toll-free 1-800-854-0303

Pleasantly landscaped site facing Disneyland. Some of the colourful bedrooms are noisy. Set rates are good value in season. 320 rooms.

Hyatt Regency Alicante ▮▮▮

100 Plaza Alicante at Harbor and Chapman
Anaheim, CA 92803
Tel. (714) 750-1234
Fax (714) 740-0465
Toll-free 1-800-233-1234

A sophisticated, ultra-modern 17-storey tower block set around a stunning atrium. Good dining and health club facilities. 400 rooms. **67**

Park Place Inn ‖

1544 South Harbor Boulevard
Anaheim, CA 92802
Tel. (714) 776-4800
Fax (714) 758-1396
Toll-free 1-800-854-8175
A sprightly motel with good-quality bedrooms. Only a few steps away from Disneyland's entrance and adjoining the fun California Bistro. 199 rooms.

Sheraton Anaheim Hotel ‖

1015 West Ball Road,
Anaheim, CA 92802
Tel. (714) 778-1700
Fax (714) 535-3889
Toll-free 1-800-325-3535
Part of a well-known chain of hotels, this peaceful, good-value establishment is built in the style of an English Tudor castle. It offers some good dining options as well as large bedrooms. 500 rooms.

Stovall's Inn ‖

1110 West Katella Avenue
Anaheim, CA 92802
Tel. (714) 778-1880
Fax (714) 778-3805
Toll-free 1-800-854-8175
Cheerful motel accommodations, a 10-minute walk away from Disneyland. There's a bar and pools on site, and a café/restaurant next door. 290 rooms.

BUENA PARK

Buena Park Hotel ‖

7675 Crescent Avenue
Buena Park, CA 90620
Tel. (714) 995-1111
Fax (714) 828-8590
Toll-free 1-800-854-8792
Pink 1970s tower block, five minutes from Knott's. Pool and good-quality bedrooms. 350 rooms.

Embassy Suites Hotel ‖‖‖

7762 Beach Boulevard
Buena Park, CA 90620
Tel. (714) 739-5600
Fax (714) 521-9650
Toll-free 1-800-EMBASSY
Buena Park's most stylish hotel. Two-room suites surround a palmy pool. Complimentary buffet breakfast and cocktails. 202 rooms.

HOLLYWOOD AND WEST HOLLYWOOD

Château Marmont ‖‖‖

8221 Sunset Boulevard
Hollywood, CA 90046
Tel. (213) 656-1010
Fax (213) 655-5311
Toll-free 1-800-242-8328
A landmark reproduction French castle set above the Strip's billboards, host to many stars. Faded rooms, with original 1920s fittings; lower floors are noisy. 63 rooms.

Holiday Inn Hollywood []

1755 North Highland Avenue
Hollywood, CA 90028
Tel. (213) 462-7181
Fax (213) 466-9072
Toll-free 1-800-HOLIDAY

A 23-storey tower block rising high above Hollywood Boulevard. Great views from the romantically lit top-floor restaurant. 470 rooms.

Radisson Hollywood [] Roosevelt Hotel

7000 Hollywood Boulevard
Hollywood, CA 90028
Tel. (213) 466-7000
Fax (213) 462-8056
Toll-free 1-800-333-3333

Hollywood institution since 1927, in Spanish Revival style. Daily TV screenings and nightly cabaret. Tower rooms face Mann's Chinese Theatre and the Hollywood sign; peaceful cabana-style accommodations enclose the pool. 335 rooms.

La Rêve []

8822 Cynthia Street
West Hollywood, CA 90069
Tel. (310) 854-1114
Fax (310) 657-2623
Toll-free 1-800-835-7997

Mainly suite hotel in a quiet backstreet – popular with long-stay movie moguls. No public rooms, but full room service and a pleasant rooftop pool. 77 rooms.

St James's Club [[] and Hotel

8358 Sunset Boulevard
West Hollywood, CA 90069
Tel. (213) 654-7100
Fax (213) 654-9287
Toll-free 1-800-225-2637

Art Deco apartment block, once home to famous movie stars and now converted into a blissful, intimate, luxury hotel. 63 rooms.

BEVERLY HILLS AND VICINITY

The Beverly Hilton [[]

9876 Wilshire Boulevard
Beverly Hills, CA 90210
Tel. (310) 274-7777
Fax (310) 285-1313
Toll-free 1-800-HILTONS

Long-established, multipurpose Hilton with rated Polynesian and French restaurants, right in the heart of Beverly Hills. Good, pleasant pool. 581 rooms.

Beverly Plaza Hotel []

8384 West Third Street
Los Angeles, CA 90048
Tel. (213) 658-6600
Fax (213) 653-3464
Toll-free 1-800-62-HOTEL

Pine-furnished bedrooms and striking Spanish restaurant in a modest hotel. Bustling Westside location. 98 rooms.

69

Hotel del Flores

409 North Crescent Drive
Beverly Hills, CA 90210
Tel. (310) 274-5115
Friendly, budget option set in a pleasant old building three blocks from Rodeo Drive. Bedrooms a bit worn, but fresh-smelling; half of them have private bathrooms. No breakfast. No pool. 36 rooms.

Four Seasons Hotel

300 South Doheny Drive
Los Angeles, CA 90048
Tel. (310) 273-2222
Fax (310) 859-3824
Toll-free 1-800-332-3442
Stunningly elegant tower block on the edge of Beverly Hills, decked out with statues, marble and soft furnishings. High proportion of suites. Gorgeous pool. 285 rooms.

Regent Beverly Wilshire

9500 Wilshire Boulevard
Beverly Hills, CA 90212
Tel. (310) 275-5200
Fax (310) 274-2851
Toll-free 1-800-545-4000
Famous, traditional hotel, with a range of expensive boutiques, piano music in the lounge and distinctively good service. Situated at the foot of Rodeo Drive – which accounts for the sky-high bedroom rates. 299 rooms.

NEAR UNIVERSAL STUDIOS

Beverly Garland Hotel

4222 Vineland Avenue
North Hollywood, CA 91602
Tel. (818) 980-8000
Fax (818) 766-5230
Toll-free 1-800-BEVERLY
Recent Holiday Inn acquisition, a three-minute drive from Universal Studios. Pleasant, leafy suburban ambience. 258 rooms.

La Maida House and Bungalows

11159 La Maida Street
North Hollywood, CA 91601
Tel. (818) 769-3857
Fax (818) 753-9363
Luxurious B&B in a 1920s suburban mansion furnished in an amazing hotchpotch of styles. Some bedrooms are in bungalows down the street. Pool and garden. Dinner on request. 11 rooms.

Sheraton Universal Hotel

333 Universal Terrace Parkway
Universal City, CA 91608
Tel. (818) 980-1212
Fax (818) 985-4980
Toll-free 1-800-325-3535
A 21-storey tower close to Universal Studios. Fun sports bar, pleasant pool. 446 rooms.

Universal City Hilton and Towers III

555 Universal Terrace Parkway
Universal City, CA 91608
Tel. (818) 506-2500
Fax (818) 509-2058
Toll-free 1-800-HILTONS
Flashy glass tower with three slick atriums, a short walk from Universal Studios. Upmarket Cantonese restaurant. 446 rooms.

NEAR MAGIC MOUNTAIN

Ranch House Inn II

27413 North Tourney Road
Valencia, CA 91355
Tel. (808) 255-0555
Fax (808) 255-2216
Toll-free 1-800-944-RHIN
Good-sized bedrooms, fun Western-themed restaurant, two pools – a 15-minute walk from Magic Mountain. 184 rooms.

Valencia Hilton Garden Inn II

27710 The Old Road
Valencia, CA 91355
Tel. (805) 254-8800
Fax (805) 254-9399
Toll-free 1-800-HILTONS
Pleasingly understated, new two-storey complex set around a courtyard with a pool. A 10-minute walk from Magic Mountain. 152 rooms.

DOWNTOWN SAN DIEGO

Hotel Churchill I

827 C Street
San Diego, CA 92101
Tel. (619) 234-5186
Basic hotel in the guise of a medieval English castle. A third of the bedrooms are themed: Jungle Safari, Circus Circus, Hawaiian Sunset ... No pool. 100 rooms.

Horton Grand II

311 Island Avenue
San Diego, CA 92101
Tel. (619) 544-1886
Fax (619) 239-3823
Toll-free 1-800-542-1886
Victorian timepiece in the Gaslamp District. The splendid bedrooms – with four-poster beds, gas fires and balconies – lie around a courtyard planted with fig trees. 132 rooms.

San Diego Marriott Hotel and Marina III

333 West Harbor Drive
San Diego, CA 92101-7700
Tel. (619) 234-1500
Fax (619) 234-8678
Toll-free 1-800-228-9290
Two gleaming, curved high rises on San Diego Bay next to Seaport village and a busy marina. Plush bedrooms, some four restaurants and a sculpted pool area. 1,355 rooms.

71

SAN DIEGO OLD TOWN

Hacienda Hotel Old Town ▓▓
4041 Harney Street
San Diego, CA 92110
Tel. (619) 298-4707
Fax (619) 298-4707 ext. 2460
Toll-free 1-800-888-1991
Hacienda-style building in heart of Old Town. Airy bedrooms below a fun Mexican restaurant. 152 rooms.

Heritage Park Bed & Breakfast Inn ▓▓
2470 Heritage Park Row
San Diego, CA 92110
Tel. (619) 299-6832
Fax (619) 299-9465
Toll-free 1-800-995-2470
Turreted Victorian house with lovingly cultivated Victoriana interior. No phone or TV in the rooms; no pool. Rates include afternoon tea and vintage film showings. 9 rooms.

MISSION BAY, SAN DIEGO

Bahia Resort Hotel ▓▓
998 West Mission Bay Drive
San Diego, CA 92109
Tel. (619) 488-0551
Fax (619) 488-7055
Toll-free 1-800-288-0770
Self-contained, mainly bungalow complex set on a tongue of land in San Diego's Mission Bay. Good pool, tennis courts, private small beach with a variety of sailboats for rent, and a pretty steamwheeler for romantic weekend cocktail cruises. 325 rooms.

Catamaran Resort Hotel ▓▓
3999 Mission Boulevard
San Diego, CA 92109
Tel. (619) 488-1081
Fax (619) 488-1619
Toll-free 1-800-288-0770
A perfectly positioned tropical-style complex situated on a sandy part of Mission Bay, only a few yards away from the mighty Pacific Ocean. Guests can take their pick from all the different types of watersports which are available on site. 315 rooms.

San Diego Hilton Beach and Tennis Resort ▓▓▓
1775 East Mission Bay Drive
San Diego, CA 92109
Tel. (619) 276-4010
Fax (619) 275-7991
Toll-free 1-800-445-8667
Extremely relaxing, well-run self-contained resort. Accommodations are plush, mostly bungalow bedrooms. Watersports, bicycle rental, tennis club and good pool available. 357 rooms.

SAN DIEGO BEACHES

The Beach Cottages   I-II
4255 Ocean Boulevard
Pacific Beach
San Diego, CA 92109
Tel. (619) 483-7440
Fax (619) 270-8819
Seventeen rustic cottages right next to the beach, with a number of less appealing apartment blocks and motel-style bedrooms at the back. Two-night minimum stay at weekends. No pool. 78 rooms.

The Bed & Breakfast   II
Inn at La Jolla
7753 Draper Avenue
La Jolla, CA 92037
Tel. (619) 456-2066
Fax (619) 453-4487
A 1913 Cubist-style house set opposite the Museum of Contemporary Art. Elegant and romantic, with carefully conceived individual bedrooms at every level of luxury. No pool. 16 rooms.

El Cordova Hotel   II
1351 Orange Avenue
Coronado, CA 92118
Tel. (619) 435-4131
Fax (619) 435-0632
Toll-free 1-800-367-6467
Pretty 1902 Spanish mansion with simple rooms. Mexican restaurant; boutiques. 40 rooms.

Crystal Pier Hotel   II
4500 Ocean Boulevard
Pacific Beach
San Diego, CA 92109
Tel. (619) 483-6983
Toll-free 1-800-748-5894
Two- to three-night minimum stays and early reservations needed for these blue and white weatherbeaten cottages strung over the ocean on a lovely old pier. All with kitchenette and private deck. No pool. 24 cottages.

Hotel del Coronado   III
1500 Orange Avenue
Coronado, CA 91118
Tel. (619) 522-8000
Fax (619) 522-8262
Toll-free 1-800-HOTEL-DEL
Famous, old-fashioned grand hotel on the beach. Ocean-view rooms are much more expensive; rooms in the newer blocks much duller (see also p.95). 691 rooms.

La Valencia Hotel   III
1132 Prospect Street
La Jolla, CA 92037
Tel. (619) 454-0771
Fax (619) 456-3921
Toll-free 1-800-451-0772
One of California's most civilized hotels. Beautiful terraces, gardens and pool. Hand-painted beams and bedrooms furnished with antiques. Three restaurants. 100 rooms.

73

Recommended Restaurants

For the best dining options within the theme parks, see pp.110-12. Listed below are some of the better places to dine just outside the parks' gates; get your hand stamped as you leave and return to the park regenerated and ready for more thrills and spills. We also recommend restaurants in Anaheim, Los Angeles (around Hollywood and Beverly Hills) and San Diego, and their nearby beach resorts. These include some of southern California's finest restaurants, as well as burger joints and pizza parlours. Restaurants are open all year round – book in advance for the most famous or popular establishments, particularly on weekends.

Price ranges are per person for a full meal, excluding drinks, tip and sales tax. (Orange County levies a 7.75% sales tax, Los Angeles an 8.25% sales tax, and San Diego a 7.75% sales tax.)

▌▌▌	Over $40
▌▌	$20-40
▌	Under $20

ANAHEIM

Belisle's ▌
12001 Harbor Boulevard
Garden Grove
Tel. (714) 750-6560
Enormous platters of excellent, all-American fare served on formica-topped tables to the accompaniment of classical music.

Flakey Jakes ▌
101 East Katella Avenue
Tel. (714) 535-1446
Spotless, self-service eatery serving high-quality burgers, pizzas, dinner platters and delicious ice-cream concoctions.

Granville's ▌▌-▌▌▌
Steak House
Disneyland Hotel
1150 West Cerritos Avenue
Tel. (714) 956-6402
Plush upmarket dining room serving all-American cuisine in the conveniently located Disney Hotel.

Monorail Café ▌
Disneyland Hotel
1150 West Cerritos Avenue
Tel. (714) 956-6402
Splendid diner set right next to the Disneyland monorail. Here you'll find breakfasts, a variety of sandwiches, shakes and burgers, and platters of American fare.

Mr Stox ‖

1105 East Katella Avenue
Tel. (714) 634-2994
Formal restaurant, popular with locals, serving an eclectic range of European and Californian dishes. Outstanding wines.

Overland Stage ‖

Inn at the Park Hotel
1855 South Harbor Boulevard
Tel. (714) 750-1811
Wild game combos and 16oz steaks in a fun, Old West atmosphere.

Shipyard Inn ‖

Disneyland Hotel
1150 West Cerritos Avenue
Tel. (714) 956-6402
Seafood restaurant and raw bar with a winning ambience, overlooking the hotel's marina.

Spaghetti Station ‖

999 West Ball Road
Tel. (714) 956-3250
Jolly, rustic Western ranch, complete with saloon, old rifles and even life-size cowboy and Indian figures.

Thee White House ‖

887 South Anaheim Boulevard
Tel. (714) 772-1381
Utterly surprising, cosy Victorian mansion offering a mixture of formal dining and sophisticated northern Italian cuisine.

Tony Roma's ‖-‖

1640 South Harbor Boulevard
Tel. (714) 520-0200
A civilized outlet of the chain that's been judged to offer 'the best ribs in America'. Opposite Disneyland entrance.

BUENA PARK

Mrs Knott's Chicken Dinner Restaurant ‖

8039 Beach Boulevard
Tel. (714) 827-1776
Family restaurant with bargain set meals. Famous for its fried chicken and boysenberry pies. Situated right outside Knott's Berry Farm. See also p.9.

Po Folks ‖

7701 Beach Boulevard
Tel. (714) 521-8955
Homestyle cooking in a kid-oriented establishment, complete with working trains, toys and a play area. Next to Movieland Wax Museum.

ORANGE COUNTY COAST

The Beach House ‖

619 Sleepy Hollow Lane
Laguna Beach
Tel. (714) 494-9707
Casual, popular seafood restaurant, directly over the beach.

75

Five Crowns   II

3801 East Coast Highway
Corona del Mar
Tel. (714) 760-0331
Tasteful reproduction of (allegedly) England's oldest inn. Specialities include roasts.

Hard Rock Café   I

451 Newport Center Drive
Newport Beach
Tel. (714) 640-8844
Surf boards may outnumber guitars on the walls, but otherwise expect the traditional Hard Rock fare of loud music and good-value burgers. Next to Fashion Island.

Planet Hollywood   I

1641 West Sunflower, Santa Ana
(at South Coast Plaza)
Tel. (714) 434-7827
Razzmatazz atmosphere for staple American/Italian food amid intriguing movie memorabilia.

Ruby's   I

#1 Balboa Pier (off Newport
Boulevard on Balboa
Peninsula), Balboa
Tel. (714) 675-7829
The best located of this endearing and spotless chain of 40s-style diners. The burgers (at least 13 types) and milkshakes (ranging from Peanut Butter to Black Forest) are simply to die for.

Splashes and   II-III
Towers Restaurant

Surf and Sand Hotel
1555 South Coast Highway
Laguna Beach
Tel. (714) 497-4477
Two top restaurants in one hotel, both right over the beach. Towers serves French/Northern Italian cuisine; Splashes offers al fresco dining and Mediterranean dishes.

HOLLYWOOD AND WEST HOLLYWOOD

Le Chardonnay   III

8284 Melrose Avenue, L.A.
Tel. (213) 655-8880
Stunning Art Nouveau salon serving light French cuisine.

Musso & Frank   II

6667 Hollywood Boulevard
Hollywood
Tel. (213) 467-7788
Old-fashioned grill (established in 1919) that refuses to change with the times. Great for roasts, steaks, fish, pasta and traditional puddings.

The Old   I
Spaghetti Factory

5939 Sunset Boulevard, Hollywood
Tel. (213) 469-7149
Massive family restaurant holding a whole railway carriage and decked out with purple velvet. Italian food.

Pink's Famous Chili Dogs

709 North Brea Avenue
(at Melrose Avenue), L.A.
Tel. (213) 931-4223
L.A.'s best known hot-dog stand, with parking lot and a little café. This is where Sean Penn is said to have proposed to Madonna.

Spago

1114 Horn Avenue at Sunset Boulevard, West Hollywood
Tel. (310) 652-4025
Hordes of celebrities, and unequalled California cuisine: Wolfgang Puck's Spago is L.A.'s most famous restaurant. Reserve.

BEVERLY HILLS AND VICINITY

California Pizza Kitchen

207 South Beverly Drive
Beverly Hills
Tel. (310) 275-1101
Also at 121 North La Cienega Boulevard (Beverly Center)
Tel. (310) 854-6555
Pizzas and pasta dishes served in a chain of sunny dining rooms.

Canter's

419 Fairfax Avenue, L.A.
Tel. (213) 651-2030
Great value, classic 24-hour deli near the Farmer's Market. Tradi-tional Jewish fare, doorstopper sandwiches and immense plates of food for big appetites.

Ed Debevic's

134 North La Cienega Boulevard
Beverly Hills
Tel. (310) 659-1952
Extraordinary 50s-style diner with all-singing and all-dancing waiters dressed to kill, and a permanent party atmosphere.

Farmer's Market

6333 West Third Street, L.A.
An attraction in its own right, with a host of colourful open-air fruit and vegetable stalls and at least two dozen ethnic kitchens. Among the best are Kokomo, a popular diner hangout, and the self-service Cajun-Creole Gumbo Pot.

The Grill

9560 Dayton Way, Beverly Hills
Tel. (310) 276-0615
A civilized but relaxed masculine dining room, just off Rodeo Drive.

Hard Rock Café

8600 Beverly Boulevard
Beverly Center, L.A.
Tel. (310) 276-7605
Burgers and rock'n'roll, music and memorabilia – not forgetting Elvis' landmark cadillac sticking out of the roof.

77

Nate 'n Al's
414 North Beverly Drive
Beverly Hills
Tel. (310) 274-0101
A famous deli where Beverly Hills folk let their hair down. Splendid, indomitable waitresses.

NEAR UNIVERSAL STUDIOS

Fung Lum
222 Universal Terrace Parkway
Universal City
Tel. (818) 763-7888
Vast Chinese restaurant in a pagoda palace, a two-minute walk from Universal Studios.

Gladstone's
Universal CityWalk, Universal City
Toll-free 1-800-GL-4-FISH
The younger sister of Pacific Palisades' Gladstone's (see p.79) is an extremely popular fish restaurant set in a colossal warehouse. Sawdust on the floor, tanks of live shellfish and an antique diving bell add to the atmosphere. Comprehensive menu; big portions.

Upstart Crow
Universal CityWalk
Universal City
Tel. (818) 763-1811
Coffees, cakes and sandwiches in an ever-so-civilized bookshop.

Victoria Station
100 Universal Terrace Parkway
Universal City
Tel. (818) 622-8180
Good American fare in an English train-station setting. Directly outside Universal Studios.

Wolfgang Puck Café
Universal CityWalk
Universal City
Tel. (818) 985-WOLF
Outlandish California-style pizzas in primary-coloured, cubist décor.

NEAR MAGIC MOUNTAIN

Marie Callender's
27630 The Old Road, Valencia
Tel. (805) 259-4675
Big, rustic family restaurant known for its choice of 33 dessert pies.

LOS ANGELES COAST

Border Grill
1445 Fourth Street, Santa Monica
Tel. (310) 451-1655
Trendy people, lots of noise and out-of-the-ordinary Mexican food.

Chinois on Main
2709 Main Street, Santa Monica
Tel. (310) 392-9025
Unique and much-praised Wolfgang Puck creation: Gallic-styled

Chinese food with suitably irreverent décor to match. Reserve.

Fish Co. ‖

174 Kinney Street, Santa Monica
Tel. (310) 392-8366
Top family seafood restaurant in an arresting converted warehouse.

Gladstone's ‖

17300 Pacific Coast Highway
Pacific Palisades
Tel. (310) 573-0212
The original Gladstone's is a vast fish restaurant right on the edge of the Pacific. (See also p.78.)

Granita ‖-‖‖

23725 West Malibu Road in the
Malibu Colony Plaza, Malibu
Tel. (310) 456-0488
One of Wolfgang Puck's latest triumphs: exotic California cuisine in a dining room styled to resemble an underwater grotto.

DOWNTOWN SAN DIEGO

Croce's ‖-‖

802 Fifth Avenue
Tel. (619) 232-2891
Trendy nightspot in the Gaslamp District, offering two sidewalk restaurants which serve Californian food, as well as rhythm and blues and jazz bars.

The Fish Market ‖-‖ and Top of the Market

750 North Harbor Drive
Tel. (619) 232-3474
Downstairs is a big, inexpensive dining room, with an oyster and sushi bar; upstairs is more formal, serving elaborate fish dishes. Harborside setting.

The Old Spaghetti Factory ‖

275 Fifth Avenue
Tel. (619) 233-4323
Mainstream Italian food in a family restaurant (see also p.72).

Ruby's ‖

322 Fifth Avenue
Tel. (619) 595-9829
Mini Harley Davisons do circuits of this 40s-style diner.

SAN DIEGO OLD TOWN

Café Pacifica ‖

2414 San Diego Avenue
Tel. (619) 291-6666
Relaxed, romantic restaurant serving nouvelle-cuisine-style seafood.

Casa de Bandini ‖-‖

Next to Bazaar del Mundo in
Old Town State Historic Park
Tel. (619) 297-8211
Mexican fare in a very beautiful 1829 adobe building with painted **79**

ceilings and walls. Always inundated with tourists.

BALBOA PARK, SAN DIEGO

Café del Rey Moro

1549 El Prado
Tel. (619) 234-8511
Lunchtime and pre-theatre Mexican and international dishes served in a lovely Balboa Park building (behind the Visitor Center). There is also an atmospheric piano bar.

Hob Nob Hill

2251 First Avenue
Tel. (619) 239-8176
Down-to-earth neighbourhood restaurant. Friendly waitresses serve large helpings of home cooking.

SAN DIEGO BEACHES

Chez Loma ▮▮

1132 Loma Avenue, Coronado
Tel. (619) 435-0661
Charming small French restaurant in a Victorian gabled house.

Firehouse Beach Café ▮

722 Grand Avenue, Pacific Beach
Tel. (619) 272-1999
A lively, family restaurant offering a multifaceted menu (breakfasts, sandwiches, burgers, Mexican and fish dishes). Popular rooftop patio.

George's at the Cove ▮▮-▮▮▮

1250 Prospect Street, La Jolla
Tel. (619) 454-4244
Outstanding California cuisine in a modernist setting, overlooking La Jolla Cove. Inventive bistro fare served in the fashionable café.

Peohe's ▮▮

1201 First Street, Coronado
Tel. (619) 437-4474
Hawaiian and American cuisine amid waterfalls and pools of exotic fish, backdropped by the dramatic San Diego skyline.

The Rusty Pelican ▮▮

4325 Ocean Boulevard
Pacific Beach
Tel. (619) 274-3474
Good fish restaurant with picture windows overlooking the beach.

Sammy's California Woodfired Pizza ▮

702 Pearl Street, La Jolla
Tel. (619) 456-5222
Novel pizzas and pasta in pine and tile surroundings.

Top O' The Cove ▮▮▮

1216 Prospect Street, La Jolla
Tel. (619) 454-7779
Highly rated traditional Continental restaurant with famously good ocean views.

80

SEA WORLD

Whiskered sea lions, musta-chioed walruses, chirpy dol-phins and sleek killer whales are the main attractions of Sea World, a marine park which takes you right up close to the ocean's most lovable and awe-some creatures, and gets them to perform some remarkable feats. Here, even the strollers are dolphin-shaped.

The park stands in a lovely setting on the shores of Mis-sion Bay, under an open sky and the 320ft (97m) landmark Skytower. The most exposed of California's parks bears the full brunt of the summer sun, while winter days can prove decidedly chilly.

Plan carefully to ensure that you see each of the three regu-larly scheduled 20-minute out-door marine shows, in which wetsuited, athletic swimmers join and cajole mammals in some memorable tricks and stunts. Between the shows, you can stroke and feed cup-fuls of fish to everything from dolphins to sting rays.

Along with all the fun and games, you'll learn an enor-mous amount about marine life at Sea World. The park takes its conservation role very seri-ously, with a long-established research institute – whose mot-to is 'Rescue, Rehabilitation, Release' – and several educa-tional department.

A close encounter of the Shamu kind at San Diego's Sea World.

The Shows

Shamu, the 12,000lb (5,440kg) lovable killer whale, is to Sea World what Mickey Mouse is to Disneyland. (In fact, three whales play Shamu, which is just a stage name.) The **Shamu Show** takes place in an arena that holds 5,500 people, with a massive video screen adding underwater shots of the powerful beast going through its paces.

You get to see Shamu close up when it beaches itself at the side of the pool to say hello to the audience, but the highlight of the show comes as a trainer takes a ride on Shamu's back and erupts out of the water on its nose. Take note that Shamu causes a big splash – literally.

Bottlenose dolphins, common dolphins, pilot whales and pseudorcas appear in the **Dolphin Show**. Marvel at the amazing acrobatics as they leap into the air and twist in unison, and jump over a high rope. The **Sea Lion and Otter Show** is played for laughs on a tropical island set. The lead actors are two adorable sea lions, Clyde and Seamore, with an otter and walrus in the supporting roles. It's side-splittingly funny to watch the sea lions' anthropomorphical antics and their gestures of fear, self-congratulation and worry.

If you have time, schedule a visit to the **Bird Showplace** to marvel at over 30 trained birds from around the world. Hawks and a bateleur eagle swoop

Spoilt for Choice

It is not feasible to see **San Diego Zoo** and **San Diego Wild Animal Park** in one day. If you want to visit both you can get reduced joint admission. If you want to visit only one, the zoo is better for younger kids as they get closer to the animals, while the wild animal park appeals to a slightly older age group, particularly those who may never have seen big animals in the wild.

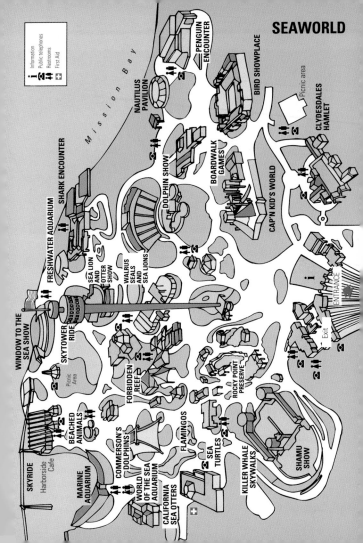

down at 100mph from an aerial balloon nearly 500ft (150m) up to land on a trainer's arm.

With so much live marine life around, **Window to the Sea Show** – a film on Sea World's research ventures and breeding programmes – may be best left to the end of your visit, if you still have time.

The Encounters

At some exhibits you're allowed to feed and touch the mammals. **Rocky Point Preserve** is the most popular, with crowds of eager servers standing nose to nose with cheery-looking dolphins, trying to fill

*S*cores of visitors enjoy the privilege of feeding the dolphins at Rocky Point Preserve.

them with cups of fish while keeping prying gulls at bay. At **Forbidden Reef**, snake-like moray eels infest the rocky habitat below ground; above, in an open pool, you can stroke harmless, velvety sting rays.

Elsewhere, you can only watch – fortunately. In **Shark Encounter**, tell-tale fins slice through the water's surface of a Caribbean-styled pool. The best place to watch sandtiger,

Tips for San Diego Zoo

Length of Visit. You need a full day to see everything, and should allow at least half a day for the highlights.

Avoiding the Lines. In summer, there can be an hour-long wait for the bus tour.

When to Visit. Any time of year is good: park hours remain roughly constant throughout the year, and there are no regular special events in summertime.

Dining. Head for the Treehouse for its upmarket café and atmospheric restaurant.

bull and lemon sharks, however, is in the highly imaginative 'submerged viewing tube'. This device allows you to walk through a giant, shark-infested pool with just a wall of plexiglass between you and flesh-ripping jaws.

Penguin Encounter is a far more sedate experience, in which a moving walkway takes you past an Antarctic landscape covered in six different breeds of penguin. You can watch the comical figures stand in huddles, waddle, preen and swim swiftly below the water's surface despite their big bellies. With time to spare, take in the otter, sea turtle and wal-rus/sea lion/seal habitats, behind the Skytower. You may want to skip Sea World's three big aquariums: there's so much else to do.

SAN DIEGO ZOO

San Diego Zoo is often hailed as the best in the world. At the last count, a phenomenal 800 species were recorded, and the zoo's endangered species programme, using sperm banks and artificial insemination, is highly enlightened.

Set within Balboa Park, the beautiful 100-acre (40ha) botanical park is densely covered in eucalypti that soar over deep **85** canyons and high mesas (hill tops). There is hardly a bar or cage in sight. Animals live in the zoological equivalent of five-star hotels behind moated enclosures. Most are grouped by type, but some species which live together in the wild have been put together in a 'bioclimatic zone'. The authenticity of this re-created habitat – down even to the appropriate sounds and humidity levels – is quite amazing. At present, the only such zone created is that of the rainforest, but over the next 20 years the whole zoo should be transformed into ten of these zones.

Despite two moving escalators that lift you up from the valleys to the hilltops, the zoo's hilly terrain makes it very tiring to get around. Take the 40-minute, open-top, double-decker bus tour the moment you enter the park, for an introduction to the flora and fauna and a witty commentary. You can select areas you want to return to on foot; sit upstairs and on the right-hand side for the best views.

Highlights

Much of the re-created rainforest area lies on a mesa in the area called the Heart of the Zoo. **Gorilla Tropics** attempts to capture the look and feel of the African rainforest: lowland gorillas play in a vast natural habitat, where stereo speakers provide the sounds of an Afri-

*S*an Diego Zoo's residents can be observed from close up – yet there are no cages in sight.

can environment. Next door, **Pygmy Chimps**, also called bonobos, swing around a palm tree playground. African birds nestle in the free-flight, multi-level **Scripps Aviary**.

In the lush vegetation of **Tiger River** below, a fogging system fills the air with water droplets to simulate the mist and humidity of the rainforest. Displays explain what medicinal products come from the rainforest, as well as the tiger's language – a chuff for hello, a quick growl for irritation, etc. Amongst the fig trees, you can spot Sumatran tigers, Malayan tapirs, crocodiles, exotic magpies and kingfishers.

A host of hairy beasts hangs out in **Bear Canyon**, namely a spectacled bear, Manchurian brown bear, Alaskan brown bear, Ceylonese sloth bear and two polar bears (often slobbing around in their pool – the algae in it sometimes gives their coats a green tinge).

Don't miss **Sun Bear Forest**, an Asian, tropical rainforest setting with orchids and ferns, home to lion-tailed macaques and Malayan sun bears – the smallest bear in the world.

You can get right up close to the elephants and four types of rhino in **Elephant Mesa**. Nearby, cute **koalas**, rarely seen in captivity, chew away on eucalyptus leaves. In the **Reptile House**, look for a red dot on the homes of king cobras, rattlesnakes, anacondas, puff

---

Tips for San Diego Wild Animal Park

Length of Visit. You'll need the best part of a day.

Avoiding the Lines. There's usually a wait for the monorail (up to an hour in summer); take it first thing in the morning.

When to Visit. The animals are more visible when it's colder. In summer, opening hours are longer, and you can take guided night-time monorail trips. Most safaris (see p.135) operate during the summer months, too.

adders and boa constrictors to find out if they're venomous. The **Children's Zoo** has odd delights such as naked mole-rats, tree kangaroos and a wonderfully ragged pot-bellied pig in the petting paddock.

SAN DIEGO WILD ANIMAL PARK

At the wild animal park, animals come first, people second. Over 1,500 mammals and 1,500 birds live here, with over 500 new arrivals being born each year. The park is proud of its breeding successes: over 75 white rhinos have been born in twenty years, for example. In most of the 2,200 acres (some 890ha), animals are free to roam in landscaped enclosures.

The park's highlight is the 5-mile (8km), 50-minute monorail trip around the enclosures – the closest you'll get to going on an African safari without ever setting foot on that continent. Some predatory species, such as large cats, are kept in large compounds which are set around Nairobi Village, a complex of thatched huts with shops and cafés.

The Monorail

Ringed by rocky Californian uplands, the undulating green and brown valleys that make

Stunning views of animals in the wild at the Wild Animal Park. A comical shoebill stork (inset).

up the park's plains, savannahs and desert of eastern, northern and southern Africa, Asian plains and water holes, are breathtakingly beautiful. Your eye roams, trying to pick out the animals.

On your round, you may see a herd of gazelles rush by at full pelt, white rhino drink at a pool and turkey vultures hover overhead. Ostriches may run by, a herd of wildebeest shuffle past, and giraffes proceed in a stately gait. If you wonder why the cranes, hornbills and herons don't just fly away, it's because they're 'pinioned', with a few feathers removed from one wing. Seeing wildlife mingling together in near-natural landscapes makes the experience so special.

Take the monorail early or late in the day when animals are more active, and try to sit on the right of the carriage for the best views.

Kilimanjaro Hiking Trail

This peaceful, 2-mile (3km) long trail allows you to get another look at the main enclosures, but this time dawdling at leisure. The trail takes you round some of the single-species habitats of cheetahs, lions, Sumatran tigers and Indian and Asian elephants, but the habitats can be so large and the vegetation so dense that you may not see that much. The best spot is Pumzika Point, a lookout which is within the eastern Africa enclosure.

Nairobi Village

In the lovely waterfowl lagoon in the middle of the village, flamingos, parrots, egrets, pelicans and spoonbills warble and preen. Look for the hilarious shoebill stork – a very rare sight in captivity.

A wander takes you to the Animal Care Center, the Hidden Jungle – a living slice of rainforest full of birds, reptiles and butterflies in a glasshouse – and to gorillas, gibbons and meerkats. You may also catch the Bird Show, where a great variety of birds talk and swoop down from great heights, the North American animals in the Wild Animal Show, or the Elephant Show.

San Diego and Vicinity

San Diego claims to be 'America's finest city', and with an impressive harbour setting, vibrant historical downtown and superb beaches – all within a stone's throw of each other – California's second largest city works hard to live up to its high reputation. It also reflects the healthy, outdoor west coast life better than L.A. or Orange County.

Lying a short drive or trolley ride away from the Mexican border and one of Mexico's largest cities, Tijuana, San Diego also has an intriguing past, partly reflected in its well-preserved Old Town, now a State Historical Park (see p.94). The best place to start your visit is at the modern heart of the city.

DOWNTOWN

San Diego's downtown is a refreshingly lively centre, where people work, live and play. Below a crop of shiny skyscrapers, carefully lit at night to accentuate their shapes, the **Gaslamp District**, once a red light area, was restored in the 1980s to its late-19th-century best. Along 4th, 5th and 6th Avenues, modernist bistros, tapas and country and western bars, antiques shops, art galleries and coffee houses fill wrought-iron, pillared buildings. The district is at its liveliest on a weekend evening, but stick to well-lit areas. Pop into adjacent **Horton Plaza**, a dazzling, state-of-the-art open-air mall built in a fantasy of colours and architecture.

Half a dozen blocks away, the **harbour** beckons, full of fishing boats and naval vessels – a third of the US Pacific fleet is moored here. Walk the harbourfront from the marina, under the gaze of svelte tower-block hotels, past **Seaport Village**, an outdoor shopping and dining complex in the style of

A walk around San Diego's Balboa Park will uncover some stunning architecture.

an old Californian seaside village, round to the embarkation point for whale-watch trips (see p.136). An old clipper, ferry and steam yacht are also moored here.

Balboa Park

Quite aside from the zoo (see p.85), the 13 museums contained within Balboa Park are **91** reason enough to visit, but they're also outshone by their stately, serene surroundings.

Erected for two expositions in the first half of this century, the beautiful Spanish-baroque buildings along El Prado dazzle. Many of the soft-hued façades are adorned with pillars and enlivened with graceful urns and faces. Light filters through the palm trees into arcaded walkways, and a lily pond sets off a majestic botanical building.

If you fancy a bit of culture as well as a wander, you need the best part of a day to do all the museums justice. On the main plaza, the **Museum of Art** has no individual must-see works but good American, Indian, Oriental, Italian Renaissance and Spanish baroque collections, as well as a fun array of Californian abstract works. Next door, the **Timken Museum of Art** is a free treat; its small assortment of masterworks includes a stimulating series of Russian icons and highly prized Dutch paintings, including portraits by Rubens and Rembrandt.

Following El Prado eastwards, Casa de Balboa holds museums devoted to photography, San Diego history and San Diego sports, but for light relief try the **Model Railroad Museum**, where grey-haired men operate enormous, intricate working sets of southwest

Whales are not the only mammals you're likely to spot on a whale-watch cruise.

San Diego Attractions

Balboa Park Museums. For information, visit Balboa Park Visitors Center, House of Hospitality, 1549 El Prado; tel. (619) 239-0512; open 9.30am-4.30pm. Museum opening hours vary, but most open daily 10am-4/4.30pm. Prices vary from free to $6. Passport ticket to nine museums $18. Thirteen museums set in beautiful old buildings. (See pp.91-4 and below)

Old Town San Diego State Historic Park, 2645 San Diego Avenue; tel. (619) 237-6770. Open 10am-5pm, shops and restaurants open later. Free. Atmospheric, 19th-century neighbourhood. (See p.94)

Stephen Birch Aquarium-Museum, 8602 La Jolla Shores Drive, La Jolla; tel. (619) 534-FISH. Open daily 9am-5pm. $6.50 adults, $4.50 children 13-17, $3.50 children 4-12. All you ever wanted to know about the sea. (See p.96)

American railroads. The **Reuben H Fleet Space Theater and Science Center** should appeal to kids, too: all the exhibits are from the hands-on, learn-as-you-play school; Omnimax films shown on a vast dome screen take you right into the action, and there are 3-D laser shows.

Across the way, the **Natural History Museum** has fresh, educational presentations on lots of Californian phenomena, from earthquakes to fossils and deserts to whales. The best reason for visiting the anthropological **Museum of Man**, at the other end of El Prado, is to see the park's most ornate building, with its mosaic-covered dome and tower.

A 10-minute walk away, the **Aerospace Museum** offers 70 real and full-size replicas of flying machines: Leonardo da Vinci's 15th-century effort, the Wright brothers' first plane, World War I and II fighters, as well as a space shuttle. The **93**

Automotive Museum alongside has British, exotic Italian and turn-of-the-century American automobiles.

OLD TOWN

Situated between downtown and Mission Bay, just off Interstate 5, Old Town harks back to the early days of San Diego. Before the American flag was raised in 1846, the city underwent a quarter of a century of Mexican rule, prior to which it had been Spanish for some years. (San Diego was, in fact, the home of the first Spanish settlers in California.)

Old Town was the centre of San Diego until the late 1800s. Now it's a pretty suburban community with a plethora of Mexican restaurants. In the **State Park** at one end of the commercial part of town, adobes and wooden structures line a couple of streets and surround a lovely plaza. Some buildings, such as the fine Casa de Estudillo and the schoolhouse, show life as it was in the 19th century under Mexican, then early American rule, while

others are old-fashioned stores or another beautiful Mexican restaurant. Guided walks start at 2pm daily, departing from the park headquarters.

A short walk away along Juan Street brings you to **Heritage Park**, a truly splendid ensemble of seven Victorian buildings salvaged from downtown. A 'widow's walk' sits atop one roof, from where a doting wife looked out to sea for her husband.

THE BEACHES

Coronado sits on the axe-headed peninsula that encloses San Diego Bay. You can either hop across on a ferry from downtown's Broadway Pier (great for downtown views), or take the 2-mile (3km) long toll bridge. The affluent, residential village (it's called a village but actually numbers 20,000 inhabitants) has a fine, unspoilt beach backed by little dunes, perfect for sunbathing.

While you're in the area, have a good look around one of the country's most famous hotels. The turreted, wooden behemoth of the Victorian **Hotel del Coronado** is best known for its famous visitors, form heads of states and presidents to movie stars. *Some Like It Hot* was filmed here, and the Prince of Wales fatefully met his future bride – Coronado housewife Wallis Simpson – in its ballroom. For more details, search out the hotel's history gallery.

A few miles north of downtown, the 4,600 acres (1,860ha) of the aquatic sports park of **Mission Bay** (also the site of Sea World, see p.65), were once just marshland. Although the bay has none of the human interest of the beaches, it's an unequalled spot for watersports and there are some sandy spots for sunbathing. A Mississippi riverboat chugs between the resort hotels for evening cocktails and dancing.

The vast **Mission Beach** spreads along the thin strip of land between the sea and Mission Bay, the focus for a hedonistic youthful scene. Its heart is **Belmont Park**, characterized by a beautiful old-fashioned roller-coaster and a 1925 indoor pool.

The sand merges into **Pacific Beach** to the north, where there's a vibrant boardwalk at weekends and in summer.

A few miles up the coast, the resort of **La Jolla** has a very different atmosphere. The

*S*an Diego's Mission recalls the city's proud history as the first Spanish settlement in California.

fashionable beach community curls around a headland indented with little coves.

Its two main drags, Girard and Prospect Streets, offer both exclusive and down-to-earth shopping. Its highly rated Museum of Contemporary Art is closed until 1996, but you can visit its downtown branch, at 1001 Kettner Boulevard at Broadway. The **Stephen Birch Aquarium-Museum** is along the northern end of town, on cliffs above the beach. Here, various water habitats display marine life, while the museum tells you everything you ever wanted to know about the ways of the sea. Its best exhibit is a simulated submarine dive, down to the ocean depths.

Explore the luxurious Hotel del Coronado and seek out its history gallery for some fascinating anecdotes about the lives of the famous.

What to Do

Shopping

If all you're looking for are Mickey Mouse ears and a Back to The Future T-shirt, the multitude of theme park shops can fit you out. Even the most reluctant shoppers, however, should experience the wonders of Southern California's ultramodern malls.

Orange County Shopping

Costa Mesa's **South Coast Plaza**, at the San Diego Freeway and 3333 Bristol Street, 10 miles (16km) south of Disneyland, is the ultimate mall for sheer size and ostentation. The vast main complex has more outlets than you would expect to find in many large towns, as well as an outdoor village and Crystal Court – a glittering showpiece full of shops marketing witty, decorative objects. Newport Beach's **Fashion Island** (600 Newport Center Drive) is on a more manageable scale, and built in a lovely outdoor arrangement of cool, terracotta-tiled, trellised walkways and newfangled fountains. There you'll find a high proportion of fashion stores as well as a stunning farmer's market.

The closest mall of note to Disneyland is the newly built **Main Place** (2800 North Main Street, Santa Ana). A 10-minute drive southeast of Disney on the I5, it boasts mainstream department stores and some 200 boutiques.

Los Angeles Shopping

Part and parcel of the LA experience is a stroll down exclusive **Rodeo Drive** and hip **Melrose Avenue** (see pp.58 and 56). As far as malls go, try the indoor **Beverly Center**, 8500 Beverly Boulevard, and **Century City Shopping Center**, just outside Beverly Hills at 10250 Santa Monica Boulevard – a more appealing, relaxing outdoor configuration.

Santa Monica, west of L.A., is something of a shopper's

paradise. Distinctive pedestrian **Third Street Promenade**, decorated with palms and dinosaur topiaries, is an upbeat Californian version of a main street. **Santa Monica Place** is decked out in a beach décor, while in **Main Street**, offbeat yet very chic boutiques alternate with lively neighbourhood cafés and bars.

San Diego Shopping

Don't miss **Horton Plaza**, in the heart of downtown, another Californian retail vision of the future with a terrific range of shops and brazen décor. The Gaslamp District is full of intriguing antique shops and art galleries, and for some serious gift-hunting, **Seaport Village**'s boutiques on the harbourfront are ideal. **La Jolla's** Prospect Street, is promoted as San Diego's answer to Rodeo Drive – only more relaxed.

Theme Park Shopping

Disneyland: you can buy virtually anything you want imprinted with a Disney logo or

*S*hop-aholics beware! Southern California's malls conceal an irresistible range of merchandise.

character, from socks to car stickers, rulers, glasses, chocolates, cookie jars, calculators, tea pots and even ice cubes. Note that merchandise in Disneyland tends to be more expensive than in other parks.

Main Street shops are open half an hour before and after official park hours. They include: Storybook Store, for literature on all the Disney stories; Emporium, Disneyland's biggest shop, where you can get all your souvenirs in one fell scoop; Magic Shop, where comedian Steve Martin once worked; and Market House, a good old-fashioned store with quality kitchenware.

The **Adventureland** shops stock good clothing and decorations all made from natural products, and tropical shirts, beads and beachwear. **New Orleans Square** offers the best park shopping for non-Disney paraphernalia, such as antiques, cut glass, and perfumes in old-fashioned bottles.

Frontierland stocks an excellent range of Western and Native American clothing such as beaver hats, Indian smocks, colourful ponchos and leather jackets. In **Fantasyland**, seek out the original Castle Christmas Shop and Disney Villains Shop. Head for Star Trader in **Tomorrowland** if you want Star Wars merchandise.

Knott's Berry Farm: Knott's Berry Farm specializes in the unlikely combination of Western apparel, Snoopy paraphernalia, dinosaurs and jam.

For **Snoopy** lovers, Rocking Horse Toys in Camp Snoopy and Snoopy's Snapshots in California Marketplace have ties, boxer shorts, trainers, lollipops and piles of cuddly toys of the beagle and the Peanuts gang. For **Western gear**, try The General Store in Ghost Town and the large shops on Grand Avenue opposite California Marketplace.

In California Marketplace, the Berry Market and the Farm Market have row upon row of jars and gift packs of **jams**, syrups, jellies, fruit spreads, salad dressings and marinades, including many products using Knott's original boysenberry. In the Roaring '20s, DinoStore covers the **dinosaur** angle.

Universal Studios: the majority of shows and attractions have an associated stall or shop next door – such as Time Traveller's Depot for *Back to The Future* gear. In the Entertainment Center, The Emporium offers the broadest selection of merchandise in the park – **99**

from stuffed King Kongs and ETs to oscars and clapper boards. Try Screen Collectibles for movie books, posters and celebrity photos, as well as offbeat items such as Bates Motel towels.

Woody's Cast of Characters specializes in Universal's cartoon-related merchandise. For a great picture souvenir, have your face superimposed on to the body of an astronaut, pin-up beauty or body builder at Amazing Pictures in the Studio Center. Alternatively, dress up in a choice of old-fashioned costumes at Professor Bloodgood's Hollywood Portraits in the Entertainment Center.

Six Flags Magic Mountain: for Warner and Looney Tunes logo items, head for Six Flags Mercantile and Looney Tunes Superstore, the park's biggest shops, at Six Flags Plaza by the park entrance. Go to Gotham City Backlot for Batman souvenirs, and for a complete

Universal CityWalk, next to Universal Studios, showcases the best L.A. has to offer.

contrast, why not try Cyclone Bay's speciality candle and glass shops, where you can watch craftspeople at work?

Sea World: does an absolutely roaring trade in cuddly toys of its killer whales, dolphins, penguins, and even sharks. You might well choose a mammal-shaped inflatable for the pool, or an original Shamu souvenir (how about a Shamu water-proof golf-club cover?).

San Diego Zoo and San Diego Wild Animal Park: the couple of big stores located at the entrances of both zoo and park stock high-quality merchandise. Naturally, you can buy cuddly versions of any number of the live furry creatures you might have fallen in love with. There's also plenty of educational games, grown-up literature about animals, conservation and the environment, and ethnic pottery, models and figurines.

Clothing is a cut above the theme park average too, with rainforest T-shirts, safari hats and zoo-keeper uniforms.

Nightlife

In summer, the theme parks keep you entertained until late into the night with laser shows and fireworks displays. Out of season, however, you'll need to look elsewhere.

Near Disneyland and Knott's are the two-hour long, fantasy-filled, family-oriented dinner shows, Medieval Times and Wild Bill's Wild West Dinner Extravaganza.

Medieval Times is probably the better of the two. Its battlements hide a sinister Museum of Torture, complete with gruesome reproductions of an executioner's axe and the rack. The main action, however, takes place in a large indoor arena. As you're gnawing your way through a whole spring chicken, a larger-than-life master of ceremonies guides you through the tournament, in which knights on horseback deftly lance hoops and spear targets before taking part in a bit of jousting and hand-to-hand combat. The skill factor is extremely high, and some of the stunts are quite dazzling. **101**

At **Wild Bill's Wild West Dinner Extravaganza**, you might be called upon to act as sheriff and serve the range stew and beans, as rope tricks, Indian dances and French can-can are performed in the arena. You'll also be expected to jeer and cheer with your fellow diners. Both venues are just down the road from Knott's: call 1-800-899-6600 for Me-

Handfuls of chicken and family entertainment – a great combination at Medieval Times.

dieval Times and 1-800-883-1546 for Wild Bill's.

In **Los Angeles**, take a walk on the wild side down Sunset Strip on a weekend night, taking in its famous rock clubs (see p.55), or search out the many offbeat venues throughout West Hollywood. High culture vultures will also find a multitude of classical music, dance and theatre venues all around the city. (In summer, the Hollywood Bowl amphitheatre stages outdoor concerts by the Los Angeles Philharmonic Orchestra.)

Nowhere could be more appropriate than Los Angeles for a night out at the movies, and Mann's Chinese Theatre in Hollywood (see p.54) is the ideal venue. (Some people buy tickets just to view the ornate interior.) Alternatively, try one of Southern California's state-of-the-art multiplexes, such as the 18-screen complex in Universal CityWalk.

Consult L.A. weekly magazines and the *L.A. Times* (see p.127 for further details and call (213) 688-ARTS for advice and tickets).

San Diego has a highly respected arts scene, too. Its five theatres in Balboa Park include one of the nation's leading repertory theatres, and the city can also boast its own symphony orchestra, opera and ballet companies. Consult the Thursday edition of the *San Diego Union-Tribune* for the latest information.

The rejuvenated downtown Gaslamp District is buzzing on a weekend evening, with jazz clubs, discos and lively bars vying for attention.

Sports

A year-round sunny climate and the California fascination for keeping in shape means there are any number of ways to work up a sweat if you have any energy to spare after crisscrossing the theme parks.

EXERCISE

Join in with the Californian crowd: put on a pair of shorts and T-shirt and go **jogging**. Hit the boardwalks or the beaches **103**

Enjoy a solitary jog at Coronado, or join the crowds at colourful Venice Beach.

themselves. **Cycling** and **rollerblading** at leisure along the boardwalks and lanes through the sands are even more popular. Join the weekend phalanxes of skaters and cyclists by hiring equipment from beachside shops at Pacific and Mission Beaches in San Diego, or at Santa Monica or Venice.

The most popular activity in Griffith Park, north of Hollywood, is **horseback riding**, and there's also a network of taxing **hiking trails**, one of which takes you right up to the Hollywood Sign. The park headquarters, at 4730 Crystal Spring Drive, tel. (213) 665-5188, has all the details.

Griffith Park has a number of **golf** courses too, but devotees of the pitted ball are best served in San Diego (self-proclaimed Golfland USA), where no less than 83 courses beckon beginners and pros alike.

Some resort hotels (around Mission Bay in San Diego, for example) have **tennis** courts (for guests only). Disney runs a tennis club next to the Disneyland Hotel; call (714) 535-4851 for more information.

WATERSPORTS

Surfing is great fun simply as a spectator sport, and top surfing spots include Zuma Beach and Surfrider Beach at Malibu; Laguna, Newport and Hunt-

ington Beaches (California's surfing capital, a mecca for *aficionados*) in Orange County; and San Diego's Pacific and Mission Beaches.

Many beaches in Southern California have outlets renting boards and wetsuits, where you can also inquire about taking lessons.

For other **watersports**, head for Mission Bay aquatic park, San Diego. Here a bewildering number of options await, from sailing to windsurfing, water-skiing and waverunners down to powerboats, with lessons available. Facilities are clustered around the resort hotels but are open to all. Snorkellers should head for the coral of La Jolla's Underwater Park.

SPECTATOR SPORTS

Los Angeles and Anaheim can boast a better choice of major league sports teams than any other city in the United States, with two major professional **105** baseball, basketball, football and hockey teams to root for. The latest arrival to the fold is the Disney-owned (hence the name) Mighty Ducks hockey team. San Diego offers a professional baseball and football team, and is hosting the America's Cup sailing extravaganza 6-11 May 1995 (contact the Convention and Visitors Bureau, see p.135).

California's Biggest Attraction?

In the months of December and January grey whales migrate over 5,000 miles (some 8,045km) down the west coast of the United States, leaving their Arctic feeding ground to calf in the warmer seas off Baja California, before heading north again in February and March. In the short time the whales spend in California waters, you can actually spot them from the shore. All along the Californian coast, cruise boats make half-day trips out to the marine highways along which the whales travel. It's **106** much colder out on the water than on land, so do bring a sweater along.

One advantage of taking a **whale-watch trip** from San Diego is the cruise through the city's busy bay, backdropped by a quite impressive highrise downtown skyline: helicopters and speedboats buzz around, in contrast to gaggles of placid sea lions basking on buoys and submarines quietly lurking in their docks.

Even though you're almost guaranteed to see *something* of the whales, you're unlikely to see much, as boat captains try not to disturb them, keeping a hundred yards away from them if possible. If you're fortunate, however, an inquisitive fellow may nose up closer to the boat. Everyone scours the water for the tell-tale sign of blows, and then, if you're looking in the right direction, you might glimpse the arch of a 40ft (12m) back and a waggle of a fluke or tail, before the mammal disappears beneath the surface. A sighting of some playful dolphins might add to the excitement. Cruise companies are listed on p.136.

Eating Out

Certain items of information in this section will already be familiar to US residents, but have been included to be of help to visitors from overseas.

Southern California lays on an amazing cornucopia of eating places and styles of cuisine. The state is renowned for its plentiful seafood, straight from the Pacific, and its abundant, home-grown fruit and vegetables. You need only take a look at the beautifully piled rows of lush produce – watermelon, grapefuit, kumquats, baby artichokes, jalapenos, radicchios – in a farmer's market.

Restaurants vie to outdo each other in eye-catching décor – a train carriage here, an underwater grotto there – and value (see our list of recommended establishments starting on p.74). Many offer play areas and wacky memorabilia to amuse the kids, as well as children's menus.

You don't have to spend a fortune to eat well in Southern

California; some of L.A.'s best restaurants are within most visitors' budgets. Dining is a popular activity, so reservations are a must at any good restaurant, especially on weekends. Valeting is commonplace: turn up in your car at the door and an eager young gentleman will park it for you, usually for a small fee.

When to Eat

Most cafés and diners serve breakfast throughout the day. Lunch is usually much cheaper than dinner, although some upmarket dining-rooms only open in the evenings. Some places offer 'early bird specials' (bargain dinner menus), from around 5.30 to 7.30pm. Californians dine early, especially on weekdays – typically from 7.30pm onwards.

Where and What to Eat

Renowned **California cuisine** was inspired by French nouvelle cuisine in the 1970s. Its hallmarks are fresh ingredients, light, flavour-enhancing **107**

sauces, with the emphasis on presentation, added to which is a free, open-minded approach to experiment, feeding off European, American and Oriental traditions. Los Angeles boasts some of the best California cuisine, epitomized by the fêted restaurants of chef/entrepreneur Wolfgang Puck.

A full **breakfast** consists of English or American muffins, eggs, bagels, pancakes, hot griddle cakes and french toast. Alternatively, try a delicious Mexican-style breakfast of *huevos rancheros* – fried eggs smothered in salsa, served with tortillas and refried beans. Coffee is plentiful, and the orange juice should always be freshly squeezed.

Most Californians aspire to a healthy diet – **salads** appear on every menu – yet all tastes are catered for, with **fast-food outlets**, including steak houses, fried chicken and rib joints

In Southern California, al fresco dining comes hand in hand with Pacific Ocean views.

all around. Burger-and-shake-oholics should root out one of the wonderful 40s- and 50s-style diners, such as Johnny Rockets and Ruby's, present all over southern California.

Every conceivable **ethnic food** is available, too. Go to a big shopping mall for a dazzling showcase of world cuisine – and to stock up on cookies, brownies, muffins, ice creams and frozen yoghurt. Drop in on a Jewish deli for a pastrami sandwich in L.A., and visit San Diego Old Town for traditional Mexican cuisine in beautiful surroundings.

Drinks

The legal drinking age in the whole of California is 21, and cocktail lounges and night-clubs do not admit people under that age. Proof of age and identification may be required.

The best **California wines** come from the northern Napa Valley, and are usually from French grapes, such as Cabernet Sauvignon and Pinot Noir for red wine, and Chardonnay and Sauvignon Blanc for white **109** wine. Cocktails are often drunk as an apéritif or accompaniment to a meal – Margaritas especially with Mexican food.

Trendy hangouts abound in Los Angeles and San Diego, and bars down at the beach are probably the coolest of them all – many have cocktail or happy hours during the early evening with half-price drinks.

Theme Park Sustinence

Though it's completely outshone by California's great culinary spread, theme park food isn't at all bad. As well as ubiquitous burgers, fries and ice cream, you can always find fruit, healthy sandwiches and some interesting platters.

Disneyland: whatever it is you crave, from French cuisine to a Mickey Mouse-shaped peanut-butter and jelly-grape sandwich, Disneyland's got it. In **Main Street**, try the Blue Ribbon Bakery for a solid breakfast and The Plaza Inn on Central Plaza for a full-scale meal. Reservations are needed for Aladdin's Oasis, a dinner show staged in a Persian Palace in **Adventureland**.

The terraced areas on **New Orleans Square**, overlooking Rivers of America, offer the park's most picturesque dining. In the Blue Bayou, the French food is overshadowed by the romantic twilight setting, adjoining the Louisiana swamps. (This is the park's best restaurant, with table service, and you are strongly advised to reserve.)

The waterside Hungry Bear in **Critter Country** is 'Famous for the bear necessities' (mainly burgers and fries). Many **Frontierland** cafés are ideally located, overlooking the lake. Casa Mexicana, in Frontierland also, offers Mexican food. The fast-food stops in **Fantasyland** and **Tomorrowland** get very crowded, so it's best to eat elsewhere. Consider the Disneyland Hotel's restaurants, too (see p.24). No alcohol is served in the park.

Knott's Berry Farm: the perenially popular **Mrs Knott's Chicken Dinner Restaurant**, in California Marketplace, is

*T*ake a break from the thrills and spills of the parks for a spot of lunch. One thing's for sure, no one goes hungry at Disneyland.

the place to go for Cordelia Knott's version of fried chicken, served with creamy mashed potatoes and followed by boysenberry pie (akin to cherry pie). **California Marketplace** also has Knott's Family Steak House, offering good-value full meals, as well as The Farm Bakery café, for takeaway breakfasts.

In the park itself, Sutter's in **Ghost Town** bakes heavenly funnel cakes made with butter and coated with icing sugar. At the Ghost Town Grill, you

are advised that 'all six shooters must be checked in at the door'. The cantinas of **Fiesta Village** are the best place to head for tacos and nachos. At Grizzly Creek Lodge in **Camp Snoopy**, you can have beagle burgers and bump into Snoopy and his pals.

Universal Studios: the self-service dining options offer a-cut-above-average theme park fare, but they are completely overshadowed by the outstanding restaurants in the adjoining **111**

CityWalk (see pp.47, 78 and 79), and Victoria Station – a full-service restaurant which you can enter from outside or inside the park (see p.79).

Within the park, 50s-style Mel's Diner is the best-known pitstop, serving classic shakes, burgers and hot dogs. The Moulin Rouge Café has French food in a brasserie atmosphere, while La Crêpe, opposite, provides lots of interesting pancakes. Eateries around the top of the escalator in the Entertainment Center provide chicken dinners, pizzas and wine, tacos and Margaritas on outdoor terraces. You can take food into all the shows and on the tram ride.

Six Flags Magic Mountain: this park is not known for haute cuisine, but for staple American, Mexican and Italian fast food. Food Etc in Pirate's Cove is a big food court that caters to all palates. There are two service restaurants: Four Winds (Samurai Summit) serves steak-house style food, but more fun is the quaint, rustic Mooseburger Lodge in High Sierra territory, where animated moose heads talk, and waiters periodically perform The Moose Muffle (a kind of shuffle). The park is alcohol free.

San Diego Parks: San Diego's parks will feed you more than adequately, but there are no places just outside them to pop out to for a meal.

In **Sea World**, head for the Harborside Café, a waiter-service restaurant with an outdoor terrace right on the edge of Mission Bay. In **San Diego Zoo**, ignore the plethora of ordinary cafeterias near the entrance and head down to the Treehouse, perched on stilts in the centre of the park. Its terraced café serves sophisticated food, while the lovely colonial-style Albert's, on a lower level, is a proper restaurant offering elaborate salads, sandwiches and full meals (open 11am-2.30pm, reserve).

Of the number of eateries in Nairobi Village in **San Diego Wild Animal Park**, Mombasa Cooker and Kisangani Court, beside the lagoon, have the most picturesque locations.

BLUEPRINT
for a
Perfect Trip

An A–Z Summary of Practical Information

> Certain items of information in this section will already be familiar to US residents, but have been included to be of help to visitors from overseas.

A

ACCOMMODATIONS (See also CAMPING on p.116, YOUTH HOSTELS on p.139 and the list of RECOMMENDED HOTELS starting on p.66)

You will find accommodations to suit all tastes and budgets in Southern California, from cheap motels to classy, five-star hotels. Many hotels offer special weekend rates and package deals with the local theme park, so it's worth asking about these when booking your accommodations.

Luxurious hotels offer excellent amenities: a choice of restaurants, health facilities, palatial, well-equipped rooms with 24-hour room service and a concierge service. **Motels** have far fewer facilities – they may not even offer breakfast – but bedrooms, however cheap, are usually large, en suite, with a phone and TV. **B&Bs** are usually upmarket, elegant affairs: what they lack in facilities, they make up for in ambience.

In most hotels, children can stay free of charge in their parents' room, and may sometimes also eat for free. One extra person in a double room can usually be accommodated for a small charge. Add hotel taxes to the room rate (see MONEY MATTERS on p.128) and remember that parking and telephone charges can add considerably to the bill.

Reserve well in advance, especially in the school holidays and summer months. A credit card is essential for holding reservations.

Anaheim Hotels. Inexpensive motels abound in the Anaheim area. Our recommended establishments (see p.66) lie within a mile or so of Disneyland and offer package rates to the park; those on South Harbor Boulevard and in Anaheim Convention Center are within walking distance. (South Harbor Boulevard is noisy, so ask for a room at the back.)

Los Angeles Hotels. L.A. is so vast that it's best to stay as close as possible to the area you're visiting. Avoid cheap motel accommodations in Hollywood, and at the other extreme, note that many famous hotels charge a great deal more than most establishments because of their reputation and prime location.

San Diego Hotels. Downtown and Old Town hotels have good shopping and dining nearby; beach hotels and the Mission Bay resort complexes are great for chilling out and are the closest to Sea World. In addition, there are a number of very attractive B&Bs. Contact The Bed and Breakfast Directory for San Diego, PO Box 3292, San Diego, CA 92163; tel. (619) 297-3130 or 1-800-424-8303.

AIRPORTS

Los Angeles International Airport (LAX), the third busiest airport in the world, lies southwest of central L.A., 31 miles (50km) from Disneyland. Call (310) 646-5252 for information.

John Wayne/Orange County Airport, 16 miles (25km) from Disneyland, is much smaller than LAX and only handles North American flights. Call (714) 252-5200 for information.

San Diego International Airport, with just two terminals, handles North American and Mexican flights only. It lies three miles (5km) northwest of downtown San Diego. Call (619) 231-7361 for more detailed information.

Other convenient airports for domestic flights include: **Ontario Int'l Airport** (35 miles or 55km east of L.A.), tel. (714) 983-8282; and **115**

Long Beach Airport, tel. (213) 421-8293; as well as **Burbank-Glendale-Pasadena Airport**, tel. (818) 840-8840.

Airport transfer. Allow considerable time to get to LAX from anywhere around Los Angeles, especially in the rush hour. The vast majority of people pick up a rental car at the airport, but if you're nervous of tackling the infamous freeways after a long flight, consider public transport to your hotel and renting a car there.

No reservations are needed for **coach** transport. Airport Coach – tel. (714) 938-8900 or 1-800-772-5299 – operates a regular service to and from LAX and John Wayne airports and all the main hotels round Disneyland/Anaheim. **Airport Cruiser** – tel. (714) 761-3345 or 1-800-762-3353 – offers a similar service but only to and from LAX.

Reservations are necessary for the many mini-bus **shuttle** services, all offering a door-to-door service. Try **Supershuttle**: for L.A. tel. (213) 338-1111 or (818) 244-2700; for Anaheim tel. (714) 973-1100; for San Diego tel. (619) 278-8877; at LAX call 417-8988. You can also contact **Prime Time Shuttle**: for L.A. tel. (213) 558-1606 or (818) 504-3600; for Anaheim tel. 1-800-924-TIME.

Confirm the cost of a **taxi** journey before setting off. Taxis from LAX to Disneyland/Anaheim are prohibitively expensive.

C

CAMPING

Disney's Vacationland Campground, 1343 South West Street, Anaheim, CA 92802; tel. (714) 774-CAMP, a 10-minute walk from the monorail, has use of the Disneyland Hotel's facilities and offers good RV and tent facilities. Or try **Anaheim KOA**, next door at 1221 South West Street, Anaheim, CA 92802; tel. (714) 533-7720.

In San Diego, two pretty sites on Mission Bay, close to Sea World, are the family-oriented **Campland on the Bay**, 2211 Pacific Beach Drive, San Diego, CA 92109; tel. 619/581-4260 or 1-800-4-BAY-FUN and the more peaceful **Harbor Resort** (RVs only), 2727 De Anza Road, San Diego, CA 92109; tel. 619 273-3211 or 1-800-924-PLAY. In summer, book well in advance for all sites.

CAR RENTAL/HIRE (See also DRIVING on p.121 and MONEY MATTERS on p.128)

Well-known firms have reservation desks at the airport terminal and at major hotels. Rates are competitive and vary widely according to the time of year, the pick-up point and the company, so it's worth shopping around if you have the time. Check the Yellow Pages under 'Automobile Renting and Leasing'.

To rent a car, you will need a valid driving licence plus an international driving permit if your own licence is in a language other than English. You must be over 21 years old (some companies, however, set the limit at 25; others levy a daily surcharge). Agencies prefer credit card transactions, but may allow a large cash deposit as well as an advance payment.

Your own insurance may provide all the cover you need for a rental car (but do check). If coming from abroad, purchase Collision Damage Waiver (CDW) – rates quoted always exclude CDW. A car booked from abroad has some third-party liability insurance (check how much with your travel agent). When you pick up the car, the agency will offer you extended third-party liability protection for an extra charge.

When booking, establish if the rental agreement includes free unlimited mileage. Check also whether you can travel outside California, as some companies limit you to driving within the state. Finally, ask if there is a supplementary charge for any additional driver – this varies from agency to agency.

Be clear about gas (petrol) arrangements: you can usually choose to pay in advance for a full tank and return it empty, or to return the car with a full tank of petrol. (Note that it can take up to an hour to return a rented car at LAX.)

CLIMATE and CLOTHING

In **summer**, the Southern Californian heat takes its toll. Theme parks, by their very nature, are exposed spaces with little shade, so make sure to drink lots of water and use plenty of sun cream. Try not to over-expose your skin to the sun's harmful rays, and keep your head covered. This is especially important for children.

117

The infamous L.A. smog is at its worst then, a possible problem for those with breathing difficulties. Evenings are usually balmy.

Winter weather is usually fair and daytime temperatures pleasantly warm. Though this is officially the rainy season, you may not see a drop for a fortnight. Evenings, however, can get decidedly chilly.

These monthly average temperatures apply to Los Angeles and Orange County. San Diego is a few degrees Farenheit cooler throughout the year.

	J	F	M	A	M	J	J	A	S	O	N	D
Max °F	65	66	69	71	74	77	83	83	82	77	73	68
Min °F	45	48	50	53	56	59	63	63	61	57	52	49
Max °C	18	19	21	22	23	25	28	28	28	25	23	20
Min °C	7	9	10	12	13	15	17	17	16	14	11	9

Clothing. Comfortable footwear is a must, as you will walk a very long way on concrete at theme parks. In summer, daywear is T-shirt, shorts and sunglasses (and a bathing suit for the beach). In winter, T-shirt and shorts are still the norm most days, but a sweater and trousers are needed in the evening. California is famously informal: dress up only for dining in a classy restaurant.

COMMUNICATIONS (See also TIME DIFFERENCES on p.134)

Post offices. The postal service deals only with mail. Post office opening hours vary, but most open 8 or 9am to 5 or 6pm weekdays, and 8 or 9am to noon or 1pm on Saturdays. Hotels, drugstores, grocery stores and theme parks also sell stamps, but stamps bought from the post office are cheaper. US mail boxes are blue.

Telephones. The US telephone system is run by several private, regional companies. Coin- or credit-card operated phones are found in all public places and along the streets. Public phones take 5, 10 and 25 cents. For local calls, deposit 20 cents in Los Angeles and Orange County, 25 cents in San Diego, then dial the seven-digit number. You

may have to deposit more money, depending on the length of the call. For long-distance calls (these include calls from one part of L.A. to another), dial 1, the three-digit code, the seven-figure number, and follow automatic voice instructions for how much change to deposit. You may have to add extra during or after your call. For international calls, you have to deposit such a large amount of change that the extra cost of phoning from your hotel room may be worth it. As well as coin-operated phones, there are credit card payphones.

The front pages of the white phone directory give information on rates, personal (person-to-person), reverse-charge (collect) and credit-card calls.

Calls are generally cheaper from 6pm to 8am. Phoning from a private phone is cheaper than from a public one, which in turn is less expensive than from a hotel-room phone. If you're phoning from your hotel room, check the rates first. Some hotels charge for using directory assistance, calling freephone numbers, making a charge card or credit card call, or even making a non-completed call.

Toll-free numbers (800 numbers) can only be used within the US (sometimes in Canada, too), and some 800 numbers are limited to California. For toll-free calls, dial 1 first, then 800, and then the seven-figure number.

Area codes are as follows: 213 for downtown Los Angeles and Hollywood; 310 for Beverly Hills, Santa Monica, Long Beach and LAX International Airport; 818 for the San Fernando and San Gabriel valleys; 714 for Orange County; 619 for San Diego.

Operator: **0**

Local directory inquiries/area codes: **411**

Long distance inquiries: dial **1**, then **area code**, then **555-1212**

International dialling: **011 + country code + area code + phone no.**

Emergencies: **911**

Fax Services/Telegrams. Most hotels will send or receive faxes on your behalf for a fee. Photocopying firms usually offer fax services. The telegraph companies are privately run. Check with your hotel concierge or the phone directory for the closest Union or Telex office. **119**

COMPLAINTS

Theme parks like to promote themselves as trouble-free, happy places, so if you have a problem, the guest relations desk should do their utmost to resolve it. If you have a serious grievance to make about any Californian business, write to the California Attorney General's Office, PO Box 944255, Sacramento, CA 94244.

CRIME (See also EMERGENCIES on p.125 and POLICE on p.131)

Like all urban areas in the United States, there is crime in LA. However, the infamous gangland areas of South Central L.A. are well off the tourist track. Visitors should take all the usual precautions: leave valuables in the hotel safe; beware of pickpockets in crowded places and avoid dark streets and run-down areas. Don't walk along the beach or travel alone late at night, and keep your wits about you even on the streets of Beverly Hills and certainly on Hollywood Boulevard. Parts of downtown San Diego can also be a little intimidating at night.

When driving, if you are lost, pull over at an open shop or garage. Only park in well-lit areas. Lock the car and don't leave any valuables on display, or any indicators that you're a tourist (such as maps, etc). 'Carjackings' have risen throughout the country, though they usually involve pricier models.

Hotels are usually very security-conscious, providing step-by-step instructions on how to minimize the risk of being robbed or mugged.

In an emergency, phone **911**.

CUSTOMS and ENTRY FORMALITIES

Canadians only need provide evidence of their nationality. UK and New Zealand citizens no longer need a visa for stays of less than 90 days in the US, but do require a valid 10-year passport and a return or onward airline ticket. The airline will issue a visa waiver form.

Citizens of the Republic of Ireland, Australia and South Africa need a visa – check with your local US consulate or embassy and allow up to three weeks for delivery.

120

Duty-free allowance. You will be asked to complete a customs declaration form before you arrive in the US. Restrictions are as follows:

Into: **USA** (if you are over 21): 200 cigarettes or 50 cigars or 2kg tobacco, 1l of wine or spirits; **Australia**: 250 cigarettes or 250g tobacco, 1l alcohol; **Canada**: 200 cigarettes and 50 cigars and 1kg tobacco, 1.1l wine or spirits or 8.5l beer; **New Zealand**: 200 cigarettes or 50 cigars or 250g tobacco, 4.5l wine or beer and 1.1l spirits; **Republic of Ireland**: 200 cigarettes or 50 cigars or 250g tobacco, 2l wine or 1l spirits; **South Africa**: 400 cigarettes and 50 cigars and 250g tobacco, 2l wine and 1l spirits; **UK**: 200 cigarettes or 50 cigars or 250g tobacco, 2l wine and 1l spirits.

For imports into the US, a non-resident may claim, free of duty and taxes, articles up to $100 for use as gifts, including an additional 100 cigars. Both arriving and departing passengers should report any money and cheques exceeding $10,000.

D

DRIVING IN SOUTHERN CALIFORNIA
(See also CAR RENTAL/HIRE on p.117)

Los Angeles is the land of the automobile. A cat's cradle of freeways interlock over an endless grid of roads and streets. Getting around can be problematic; avoid rush hour times: 7-10am and 3-7pm weekdays. By contrast, good signposting and generally light traffic make driving around **San Diego** a pleasure. Traffic moves well around **Orange County**'s suburban sprawl, but it's very easy to get lost: cities merge into each other and signposting is poor.

The **rules** are straightforward. Drive on the right, pass on the left (except on the highway, where traffic overtakes on both sides). Drivers and all passengers *must* wear seat belts; children must be in a car seat if they weigh 40lb (18kg) or less (usually under four years of age). Rental car companies now offer these child seats for an additional fee and subject to availability. It is a serious offence to pass a school bus *in either direction* on a two-lane road when it is taking on or setting down passengers. Strict drunk-driving laws are enforced and anyone found driving under the influence of alcohol will be arrested.

For traffic reports, tune into KFWB 980-AM. For up-to-date traffic information, call CalTrans Highway Information on 1-800-427-7623.

Pedestrians. Jaywalking (crossing in the middle of the street) is illegal. You can be fined for this offence.

On the Streets. Avenues and boulevards stretch for many miles, so try and establish a cross-street reference when looking for an address. Sometimes building numbers are marked on the street signs (eg 1000-1100). Left turns off carriageways are usually made by simply getting into the middle lane. U-turns are permissible except where stated otherwise. Likewise, unless there's a sign to the contrary, you can turn right on a red light, providing you stop and check that no pedestrians or traffic deter this manoeuvre. At crossroads with no traffic lights, you take it in turns to cross. Speed limits in built-up areas are 25mph (40kph) unless otherwise stated.

Highways. High-speed divided highways are called freeways, and L.A. has the most extensive freeway system in the world. For short distances, consider avoiding the freeway route: average commuter speed during rush hours has dropped to 20mph (30kph). Before setting out, study your map and determine the exact route you intend to take. Freeways have both a number and a name, and sometimes there are two names depending on which part of the city you're in and which direction you're heading. Exits come up fast and traffic often precludes radical action. Carpool lanes (marked with diamonds) are intended for cars carrying at least two passengers. If you are caught with insufficient passengers, you may be fined. The speed limit on freeways is 55mph (90kph). Freeways are either indicated by a name, number, or both:

1	Pacific Coast Highway/PCH
5	Golden State/Santa Ana Freeway
10	Santa Monica/San Bernadino Freeway
55	Costa Mesa Freeway/Newport Boulevard

101	Ventura/Hollywood
110	Harbor/Pasadena Freeway
134	Ventura/East of Hollywood
170	Hollywood
405	San Diego

Gas (petrol) Stations. At many stations you will have to go inside and pay in advance (ask if you want to fill the tank). Gas from self-service pumps is cheaper than from assisted pumps. There are several grades of gas; regular unleaded will suffice for most rental cars, but check with the company when you pick up the vehicle.

Parking. Parking restrictions are shown by curb markings: a white line means a 3-minute maximum stop (10 minutes at hotels), 24 hours a day; a red line means no parking whatsoever; green and blue are for disabled badge-holders only. Downtown hotels make punitive charges for parking. At the massive theme park and mall car parks, make a note of where you have left the car.

Breakdowns and Accidents. If you break down in a rental car, look for the emergency breakdown number on the dashboard or in the glove compartment. Otherwise, wait for the Highway Patrol to come by, or, if you're on a freeway, head for a call box at the roadside (spaced every half-mile) which will automatically connect you with the Highway Patrol. If your car stalls in a traffic lane, turn on your emergency flashers and stay inside with your seat belt on. *Never* attempt to dash across the freeway to reach a call box.

The American Automobile Association (AAA) offers some breakdown assistance and motoring information to members of affiliated organizations abroad (check with your local organization). Contact The Automobile Club of Southern California, 2601 South Figueroa Street, Los Angeles, CA 90007; tel. (213) 741-3111. For AAA emergency road service, phone 1-800-AAA-HELP.

Distances. The distances listed overleaf should help you plan your journey. Note that the times given are approximate, and assume light traffic conditions.

123

Disneyland-Knott's Berry Farm: 6 miles (10km)/15 min.

Disneyland-Universal Studios: 35 miles (55km)/1 hour.

Disneyland-Sea World: 90 miles (145km)/2 hours.

Disneyland-San Diego Wild Animal Park: 80 miles (130km)/1 hour 45 min.

San Diego Wild Animal Park-Sea World: 30 miles (50km)/45 min.

Universal Studios-Magic Mountain: 21 miles (34km)/30 min.

Universal Studios-Sea World: 130 miles (210km)/2 hours 45 min.

Distance

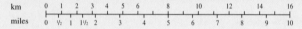

Fluid measures

EARTHQUAKES

Briefly, if you feel a tremor while you're indoors, stay there and take cover under a sturdy table or door-frame. Stay clear of windows and fireplaces. Don't rush outside. Do not try to use the stairs or elevators while the building is shaking. Outside, avoid trees, power lines and the walls of buildings. In a car, stop and sit it out by the side of the road, but away from power lines and bridges. If you want to be prepared for the worst, study the front pages of the white telephone directory.

ELECTRIC CURRENT

Throughout the US, the standard is 110-volt, 60-cycle AC. Plugs are small, flat and two-pronged. Visitors from overseas will need an adaptor.

EMBASSIES and CONSULATES

All embassies are in Washington, DC, but many countries maintain consulates in Los Angeles.

Australia: 611 North Larchmont Boulevard, Los Angeles, CA 90004-998; tel. (213) 469-4300.

Canada: 300 South Grand Avenue, 10th Floor, Suite 1000, Los Angeles, CA 90071; tel. (213) 687-7432.

Republic of Ireland: 655 Montgomery Street, Suite 930, San Fransisco, CA 94111; tel. (415) 392-4214.

South Africa: 50 North La Cienega Boulevard, Suite 300, Beverly Hills, CA 90211; tel. (310) 657-9200.

United Kingdom: 11766 Wilshire Boulevard, Suite 400, Los Angeles, CA 90025; tel. (310) 477-3322.

EMERGENCIES (See also DRIVING on p.121, EARTHQUAKES on p.124, MEDICAL CARE on p.127 and POLICE on p.131)

Call the all-purpose emergency number **911**, from any telephone; no coins are required. The operator will ask you if you want the police, an ambulance or the fire department.

G

GAY and LESBIAN TRAVELLERS

California has been at the forefront of gay politics for many years, and West Hollywood is a centre of gay and lesbian life in L.A. Phone the Gay and Lesbian Community Services Center on (213) 848-2220. Gay-oriented arts, bars and events are covered in magazines such as *Frontiers* and books such as *Bob Damron's Address Book*, available in good bookshops.

L

LANGUAGE

Spanish shop and street signs reflect southern California's large Hispanic presence – Spanish is the second language of the region. Most

English-speaking foreigners are familiar with American words or phrases, but here are a few that may cause confusion:

US	British
bill	banknote
check	bill (restaurant)
drugstore/pharmacy	chemist
faucet	tap
first floor/2nd floor	ground floor/first floor
pants	trousers
purse/pocketbook	handbag
sidewalk	pavement
stroller	pushchair
underpass	subway

LOST PROPERTY

Airports, department stores and attractions such as amusement parks have special 'lost and found' areas. If your lost property is valuable, contact the police who will have you fill out a report to reclaim your property if it is recovered. If you lose your passport, get in touch with your consulate (see p.125).

M

MEDIA

Radio and television. You'll probably be sitting in the car for some of your time in California. Here are some radio stations to tune in to in Los Angeles and Orange County: KXEZ-FM (100.3) easy listening; KKGO-FM (105.1) classical; KLSX-FM (97.1) classic rock; KLON-FM (88.1) jazz; KABC-AM (790) talk; KFWB-AM (980) constant freeway updates.

Almost every hotel room has a TV. Most hotels subscribe to cable channels, such as CNN for non-stop news, MTV for music, ESPN for sports and the Disney Channel. The nationwide commercial networks are found on channels 2 (CBS), 4 (NBC), 7 (ABC), 11 (Fox). Channel 28 (PBS) is the public broadcasting service, with no adverts and generally higher quality programmes. For San Diego, these are 8 (CBS), 39 (NBC), 10 (ABC), 6 (Fox), 15 (PBS). You'll also find Spanish-speaking stations and public access channels, showing everything from evangelical appeals to psychic hotlines.

Newspapers and Magazines are vital sources of information in the US, where convention and visitors bureaux promote only affiliated companies. Sunday newspapers are especially comprehensive. Sunday and Friday editions of *The Orange County Register* print entertainment listings. *The Los Angeles Times* has a daily Calendar section, at its fullest on Sunday. *The San Diego Union-Tribune* publishes its Night and Day entertainment section on Thursdays.

Most Orange County and San Diego magazines are geared to the visitor. They're free and available in hotel lobbies. In San Diego, look out for the bi-monthly leaflet *San Diego Performing Arts Guide*. L.A.'s free entertainment magazines (also available in hotel lobbies), such as *Entertainment Today*, *Los Angeles Reader* and *L.A. Weekly*, give a fascinating insight into city gossip and local obsessions. *Where? Los Angeles* is a good reference source aimed at the visitor. The more glossy *Los Angeles* is sold in newsagents.

MEDICAL CARE

No vaccinations are required by US health authorities, unless, of course, you are coming from known cholera or yellow fever areas.

Healthcare, especially hospitalization, is extremely expensive in the United States. Overseas visitors should therefore make arrangements before leaving home for temporary health insurance with a high level of cover. Contact a travel agent or an insurance company. Hospital emergency rooms will treat anyone in need of speedy attention.

If you do need medical assistance, call for a doctor: tel. 1-800-3627-911 for a nationwide service. Hotel staff will direct you to a suitable hospital nearby; alternatively, refer to the Yellow Pages.

Some medicines sold over the counter abroad are only available on prescription in the US – check with your doctor.

Drugstores/Pharmacies. 24-hour pharmacies include:

Sav-on, 1021 North Street Boulevard, Anaheim; tel. (714) 991-9161.

Kaiser Permanente, L.A. Medical Center, 1526 Edgemont Street, Hollywood; tel. (213) 667-8301.

Thrifty, 535 Robinson Avenue, Hillcrest, San Diego; tel. (619) 291-3703.

Theme parks are equipped with first-aid stations.

MONEY MATTERS

Currency. The dollar ($) is divided into 100 cents (¢).

Banknotes: $1 (a buck), $5, $20, $50, $100. All notes are the same size and colour, so double-check your cash before dispensing it.

Coins: 1¢ (penny), 5¢ (nickel), 10¢ (dime), 25¢ (quarter). 50¢, $1 and $2 coins are very rare.

Banks and Currency Exchange. Banks are generally open from 9am to 5pm Monday to Thursday, until 6pm on Friday and some operate on Saturday morning. Foreign travellers are advised to carry travellers' cheques and cash in dollars. You'll find Thomas Cook or American Express outlets in all major cities and at the airport.

The Bank of America, on the east side of Town Square in Disneyland, offers full banking services from 9am to 4pm daily. At almost all the theme parks, you can draw cash with a credit card at ATM machines (check with your bank for details). At Disneyland, you can change dollars for Disney dollars, available in $1, $5 and $10 denominations.

Credit Cards. Plastic is vital for hotel and car rental reservations and is the presumed method of payment for large transactions. In theme parks, however, credit cards cannot be used to purchase some items, such as fast food, for example.

Traveller's Cheques. Banks, stores, hotels, restaurants and even gas (petrol) stations usually accept travellers' cheques as the equivalent of cash *if* they are in US dollars. Traveller's cheques drawn on American banks or American Express are widely recognized. Change only small amounts of money at a time. Keep the balance of your cheques in the hotel safe and keep a note of their serial numbers.

Tax. Advertised prices (except for attractions and gas/petrol) do not include tax. All purchases, with the exception of groceries, are subject to a sales tax. Orange County levies a 13% hotel tax and 7.75% sales tax, Los Angeles a 14% hotel tax and 8.25% sales tax, and San Diego a 9% hotel tax and a 7.75% sales tax.

PLANNING YOUR BUDGET (See also THEME PARK ADMISSION PRICES on p.14-15 and HIGHLIGHTS on pp.34, 56 and 93)

Prices are higher in the theme parks than out in the real world: allow at least $20 for food and drink per person per day in a theme park, and don't forget to budget for souvenirs. Here are some guideline prices.

Airport Transfer. *Coach*: LAX-Disneyland $14 single; John Wayne-Disneyland $10 single. *Shuttle* fares are similar to coach fares. *Taxi*: LAX-Disneyland $63; John Wayne-Disneyland $25; LAX-Hollywood $24.

Babysitters. From $8 an hour.

Car Rental/hire. Typical rate for an economy car: from $100 to $250 a week with unlimited mileage, plus $70-80 a week for CDW. Child car seats are typically $5 a day, $25 a week.

Clothes. Theme park T-shirt $12-15, sweat shirt $20.

Gas (petrol) From $1.05 per unleaded US gallon (approximately 4 litres) from a self-service pump. As much as 50¢ extra a gallon if attended.

Hotels. High season rates for a double room: expensive $150 and over; moderate $80-150; budget $80. Hotel rates out of season are often considerably lower than advertised rates (eg $30 for a cheap motel room near Disneyland). (See also the list of RECOMMENDED HOTELS starting on p.66.)

Laundry. *Laundromat*: $2 for a wash and about $1.50 for drying; *service wash*: $7 a load; *hotel service*: around $3 a shirt.

Meals and Drinks. Continental breakfast $3; full breakfast $4-10; restaurant lunch $7 and up; dinner $15 (inexpensive) to $40 and up (expensive); hot drink $1-1.50; beer $2-4; glass of wine $3 and up; bottle of wine $12 and up; cocktail $4 and up. *Theme park costs*: sandwich $5; main dish $6-9; frozen yoghurt/ice cream/soft drink $1.50-2. **129**

Parking. At theme parks usually $5. Upmarket Los Angeles and San Diego hotels $8-15 a day.

Photography, Video. Colour film (36 exposures) $5.50 from drugstore. *Theme park prices*: colour film $6.50; disposable camera (27 exposures) $10-12; blank video cassette $8-10; camera rental free to $5; video camera rental free to $40. (Note that tapes made for the US market won't work on European systems and conversion is expensive.)

Sports Equipment Rental. Bicycle, rollerblade, rollerskate, surf board, wetsuit rental: $4 an hour, $10 a day. Sail boats $20 an hour. Powerboats and waverunners $50 and up for an hour.

Stroller/Pushchair Rental. At theme parks, usually $5.

Taxis. From $1.20-1.90 for pick-up; around $1.60 a mile.

Tickets. Cinema up to $7.50. Dinner and show $30 and up. Theatre $10-65. TV shows free. Baseball $5-11. Basketball $10-35. Football $15-30. Hockey $13-125.

Tours. Film studio tours $10-$25. Three-hour Hollywood/Beverly Hills tour $25.

Whale-Watching Cruises. Around $15 adults, $7.50 children.

Wheelchair Rental. At theme parks, usually $5.

OPENING HOURS

For theme park opening hours, see p.14. For opening hours of other attractions, see p.34 for Orange County, p.56 for Los Angeles and p.93 for San Diego.

Banks. Generally open Mon-Thurs 9am-5pm, until 6pm on Friday; some operate on Saturday morning.

Shops. Main street shops are usually open Mon-Sat 10am-6pm; shopping malls Mon-Fri 10am-9pm, Sat 10am-6 or 7pm, 11am-6pm Sun. 7-Eleven grocery stores are open 24 hours a day.

PHOTOGRAPHY and VIDEO

Drugstores and supermarkets sell film at lower prices than specialist camera shops and theme parks. Pre-recorded tapes bought in the US do not run on European videos systems (and vice versa), nor will the tapes you make on rented equipment – and conversion is expensive.

All theme parks stock film, video cassettes and disposable cameras, and most provide a speedy developing service. All the parks will rent (sometimes just for the price of buying a film) still cameras. Disneyland, Universal Studios and San Diego Zoo and Wild Animal Park rent out video cameras on the basis of a credit card deposit.

POLICE (See also EMERGENCIES on p.125)

In an emergency, phone the all-purpose emergency number, **911**. City police deal with crime and offences within their district. Highway Patrol officers or State Troopers man the highways and freeways, and issue speeding tickets.

PUBLIC HOLIDAYS

When certain holidays (such as Christmas) fall on Sunday, banks, post offices and most stores close on the following Monday. They close on Friday if those holidays fall on a Saturday.

New Year's Day	1 January
Martin Luther King Jr Day	Third Monday in January
President's Day	Third Monday in February
Memorial Day	Last Monday in May
Independence Day	4 July
Labor Day	First Monday in September
Columbus Day	Second Monday in October
Veterans' Day	11 November
Thanksgiving	Fourth Thursday in November
Christmas Day	25 December

131

RELIGIOUS SERVICES

Hotels can direct you to your nearest church, temple, synagogue or mosque. Alternatively, look in the Yellow Pages or in the Saturday newspapers, which provide information on Sunday services.

SMOKING

Smokers are pariahs in Southern California, and smoking is banned altogether in Los Angeles restaurants. Laws vary in surrounding communities, but all restaurants must have a non-smoking section. Theme parks do not permit smoking on rides or in eating areas.

TICKETS (See also TOURS on p.135)

The hotel concierge service is the first port of call for assistance in obtaining tickets to cultural and sporting events. You can also contact **Ticketmaster** (714) 740-2000 Orange County; (213) 480-3232 Los Angeles; (619) 278-8497 San Diego. In Los Angeles, call (213) 688-2787 for the latest information on arts in the city. The L.A. Arts Passport, available from the Los Angeles Convention and Visitors Bureau, offers big savings at many theatres and arenas. In San Diego, Times Arts Tix Center, Broadway Circle at Horton Plaza Park, tel. (619) 238-3810 (Tues-Sat 10am-7pm), issues half-price day-of-performance tickets for cash only and full price advance tickets. The front of the Yellow Pages lists contact numbers for ticket inquiries.

Baseball (Apr-Sept): *California Angels*, Anaheim Stadium, tel. (714) 634-2000; *Los Angeles Dodgers*, Dodger Stadium, Los Angeles, tel. (213) 224-1400; *San Diego Padres*, San Diego Jack Murphy Stadium, tel. (619) 283-4494.

Basketball (Nov-May): *Los Angeles Clippers*, L.A. Sports Arena, tel. (213) 748-8000; *Los Angeles Lakers*, The Great Western Forum, Inglewood, tel. (310) 419-3160.

Football (Aug-Dec): *Los Angeles Raiders*, Los Angeles Memorial Coliseum, tel. (310) 322-5901; *Los Angeles Rams*, Anaheim Stadium, tel. (714) 937-6767; *San Diego Chargers*, San Diego Jack Murphy Stadium, tel. (619) 280-2111.

Hockey (Oct-Apr): *Los Angeles Kings*, The Great Western Forum, Inglewood, tel. (310) 419-3160; *Mighty Ducks of Anaheim*, Anaheim Arena, tel. (714) 704-2400.

Studio Tours and TV Shows. Many television shows are taped before a live, studio audience. You can obtain tickets by writing to the studio and identifying the show you would like to see and the date of your visit (include a self-addressed, stamped envelope). Tickets are also available on the day from the studio guest relations office. A ticket doesn't assure you of a seat, as more tickets are issued than there are seats available, so get in line as early as possible for any show. Most shows don't allow children under the age of 10, others set a limit at 16 or 18. *Hollywood Reporter* details TV shows and films in production.

Audiences Unlimited, 100 Universal City Plaza, Building 153, Universal City, CA 91608; tel. (818) 506-0067 for show schedules and tickets covering most studios, including Universal Studios. Shows include *Coach* and *Martin*. Box offices at Fox TV Center, 5746 Sunset Boulevard and in Universal Studios park.

ABC-TV, 4151 Prospect Avenue, Hollywood, CA 90027; tel. (213) 520-1ABC. Shows include *America's Funniest Home Videos*.

CBS-TV, 7800 Beverly Boulevard, Los Angeles, CA 90036; tel. (213) 852-2624. Shows include *The Price is Right*.

NBC-TV, 3000 West Alameda Avenue, Burbank, CA 91523; tel. (818) 840-3537. Shows include *The Tonight Show*; one-hour tours Mon-Fri 9am-3pm, Sat 10am-4pm. $6.75, $3.75 children 5-12.

Paramount Studios, 860 North Gower Avenue, Hollywood, CA 90038; tel. (213) 956-5575. Shows include *The Arsenio Hall Show*, **133**

Fresh Prince of Bel Air; two-hour walking tour weekdays 9am-2pm $10; under-10s not admitted.

Warner Bros, 4000 Warner Boulevard, Burbank; tel. (818) 954-1744. Tickets for shows (including *Murphy Brown*) available through Audiences Unlimited; two-hour tours 10am-3pm. $25 (reserve); under-10s not admitted

TIME DIFFERENCES
The continental United States is divided into four time zones. California is in the Pacific zone, which is 8 hours behind GMT. Daylight saving time is adopted from the first Sunday in April and the last Sunday in October, when the clocks move forward one hour (GMT -7 hours).

Los Angeles noon (Sun)	New York 3pm (Sun)	London 8pm (Sun)	Sydney 6am (Mon)	Jo'burg 10pm (Sun)

TIPPING
You are expected to add about 15 percent to restaurant and bar bills, based on the grand total of the bill, including tax. If service has been exceptionally good, 20 percent is appropriate. In cafés where you pay the cashier on the way out, leave the tip on the table. In a bar, leave the change on the bar top, and tip as you would in a restaurant for table service.

Cinema or theatre ushers are not tipped, but doormen, cloakroom attendants, etc, should be remunerated – no less than 50 cents. It is customary to tip the parking valet when he brings your car around for you (but not when he parks it). Some suggestions:

Tour guide	10-15%
Hotel porter	$1
Taxi driver	15%
Valet	$1
Waiter/waitress:	15-20%

TOURIST INFORMATION OFFICES

For visitors from abroad, general information about travel in the US is available from the United States Travel and Tourism Administration in your own country. On the spot, hotels usually have a good stock of leaflets and brochures for nearby attractions. For more information on the theme parks, refer to the addresses and phone numbers listed on pp.14-15.

Anaheim Convention and Visitors Bureau, 800 West Katella Avenue, PO Box 4270, Anaheim, CA 92803; tel. (714) 999-8999; open Mon-Fri 8.30am-5pm. Not really geared to walk-in inquiries.

Los Angeles Convention and Visitors Bureau, 633 West Fifth Avenue, Suite 6000, Los Angeles, CA 90071; tel. (213) 689-8822. Ask for the seasonal *Destination Los Angeles* booklet.

Hollywood Visitor Information Center, Janes Square, 6541 Hollywood Boulevard; tel. (213) 689-8822; open Mon-Sat 9am-5pm.

Beverly Hills Visitors Bureau, 239 South Beverly Drive, Beverly Hills; tel. (310) 271-8174; open Mon-Fri 8.30am-5pm.

San Diego Convention and Visitors Bureau, 401 B Street, Suite 1400, Dept 700, San Diego, CA 92101-4237; tel. (619) 232-3101. Ask for the seasonal *Official Visitors Guide*.

For walk-in inquiries, visit the excellent **San Diego Visitor Information Center**, First Avenue and F Street, 11 Horton Plaza; tel. (619) 236-1212; open Mon-Sat 8.30am-5pm, Sun in summer 11am-5pm.

TOURS
(See also STUDIO TOURS and TV SHOW TICKETS on p.133)

Theme Park Tours. For an increased admission charge, **Disneyland** offers a 3-hour-long guided tour giving an overview of the park. At **Seaworld**, you can go on an inexpensive 90-minute educational tour to see animal care facilities and training centres. Those over 12 years of age can make costly but exciting forays on open-air vehicles into the **San Diego Wild Animal Park** enclosures. These take place from May to September and on the first weekend of the month from October to April. Reserve a month in advance on (619) 738-5022. **135**

Sightseeing Tours. A host of companies from Anaheim and Los Angeles offer a range of coach and minibus tours, from theme park trips to sightseeing trips round Hollywood, Beverly Hills (see p.59) and the beaches. Try: **Oskar J's**, tel. 1-800-OSKAR-01; **Odyssey Sightseeing**, tel. (714) 939-1001; **Gray Line** tel. (714) 978-8855 Orange County, (213) 856-5900 Los Angeles, (619) 491-0011 San Diego. A good way to see San Diego is on the **Old Town Trolley Tours**, tel. (619) 298-8687), which allow you to get on and off as you please.

Whale Watching. Many companies offer whale-watching cruises (December-March). Most also provide harbour cruises, dinner cruises and deep-sea sportsfishing. Try: **Long Beach**: Catalina Cruises, 320 Golden Shore Boulevard, tel. 1-800-228-2546. **Newport Beach**: Balboa Pavilion, 400 Main Street, Balboa, tel. (714) 673-1434; Hornblower, 2431 West Coast Highway, tel. (714) 646-0155. **San Diego**: San Diego Harbor Excursion, 1050 North Harbor Drive, tel. 1-800-442-7847; Hornblower, 1066 North Harbor Drive, tel. (619) 234-8687; Islandia Sportfishing, 1551 West Mission Bay Drive; tel. (619) 222-1164.

TRANSPORT (See also CAR RENTAL on p.117, DRIVING IN SOUTHERN CALIFORNIA on p.121 and TRAVELLING TO SOUTHERN CALIFORNIA on p.137).

Travelling by **car** is still the easiest way to get from A to B in Southern California. Many hotels lay on a free **shuttle** to the local theme park. Free shuttles also visit shopping malls in Orange County. **Taxis** are plentiful outside the hotels and malls, but they rarely respond to being hailed on the street. Of the many taxi firms, Yellow Cab Company operates in Orange County, tel. (714) 535-2211; Los Angeles, tel. (213) 483-9001; and San Diego, tel. (619) 234-6161.

Public transport. Orange County Transportation Authority (OCTA) operates the many **bus** routes in the county: call (714) 636-RIDE. The Southern California Rapid Transit District (RTD) covers Los Angeles with many bus routes, reaching the beaches and most sights: tel. (213) 626-4455; don't travel on them at night. The DASH **shuttle** system **136** operates in downtown L.A. during the daytime. DASH systems also operate in Hollywood, Westwood and other areas of the city. A similar shuttle system, the Runabout, operates in Long Beach.

San Diego has a good transport system, with a **trolley** from downtown to the Mexican border, and **buses** that take you to and from all the major attractions, beaches and hotels. One- and four-day passes are available. Call (619) 234-3004 for details.

TRAVELLERS WITH DISABILITIES

Accessibility and facilities for the disabled are excellent in southern California. At the theme parks, special parking, wheelchairs and wheelchair-accessible toilets are on hand. For some attractions, guests can remain seated in their wheelchairs. Disney publishes a *Guidebook for Guests with Disabilities*. For visitors with visual impairments, City Hall stocks audio-cassette tape tours. Inquire at guest relations in all the parks for advice – Knott's Berry Farm, Universal Studios and San Diego Wild Animal Park also produce information booklets.

The Junior League of Los Angeles distributes a guide for the disabled outlining the wheelchair facilities of the area's most popular sites and attractions. For a copy of 'Around the Town with Ease', send $2 for postage and handling to the league at Farmers Market, Third and Fairfax, Los Angeles, CA 90036 or call (213) 937-5566 for more information.

For San Diego attractions and hotels, get *Accessible San Diego* from 2466 Bartel Street, San Diego, CA 92123; tel. (619) 279-0704.

TRAVELLING TO SOUTHERN CALIFORNIA

FROM NORTH AMERICA

By Air. Direct flights operate from major US and Canadian cities to Los Angeles International Airport (LAX). There are also direct flights from some cities to John Wayne Airport and San Diego International Airport, which are both more pleasant alternatives to LAX and more convenient for most of the theme parks.

By Bus. Southern California is linked to all major cities by Greyhound; call them on 1-800-231-2222. Foreign travellers can purchase an Ameripass – which must be bought outside the US – for unlimited **137**

travel within a set period. Phone the Greyhound representative in your own country.

By Rail. Major Amtrak routes run across the country to Los Angeles. The so-called Californian Corridor runs south through Anaheim to San Diego. Call 1-800-USA-RAIL for more information. Overseas visitors can purchase rail passes for unlimited travel within a set period of time. The Coastal and West Region rail passes, for example, cover southern California. Contact the Amtrak sales representatives in your country.

FROM OVERSEAS

Direct flights from abroad fly into Los Angeles International Airport (LAX). Air fares cost more in summer and at peak periods like Christmas. Airlines' APEX fares are usually their cheapest, but carry restrictions such as needing to be purchased at least 21 days in advance. Consolidated fares (available from 'bucket shops') usually offer the best bargains.

From the UK (10 hours). Major airlines fly direct from Heathrow and Gatwick – flights are either non-stop or with one stop – and from Manchester (in summer). Otherwise, routing from regional airports is via London or an American city.

From the Republic of Ireland (13 hours). There are no direct flights from Dublin; routing is either through an American city or London.

From Australia (13½ hours) **and New Zealand** (12 hours). There are direct flights from Sydney and Auckland.

From South Africa (23 hours). There are no direct flights from Johannesburg. Routing is via Miami, New York or London.

Packages. Many tour operators offer all-inclusive packages, including flight, car rental, accommodations and theme park tickets. Inquire at your local travel agent.

Air passes. Overseas visitors wishing to make **domestic** flights within the US can save a considerable amount by buying an air pass *before* reaching the country. These are offered by most major airlines.

WEIGHTS and MEASURES

For fluid and distance measures, see p.124. Efforts to ease the US into the metric system are proceeding slowly. In real life, however, it's still inches, feet, yards, miles and degrees Fahrenheit.

Weight

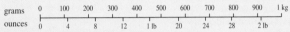

Length

Temperature

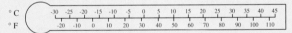

YOUTH HOSTELS

YMCA/YWCA, AYH and private hostels can all be found in Los Angeles, the beach resorts and San Diego. For AYH details, contact your national youth hostel association. Alternatively, write to:

AYH Los Angeles Council, 1434 2nd Street, Santa Monica, CA 90401, tel. (310) 393-3413.

AYH San Diego Council, 335 West Beech Street, San Diego, CA 92101, tel. (619) 239-2644.

Index

Where there is more than one set of references, the one in **bold** refers to the main entry. Page numbers in *italic* refer to an illustration.

143

Berlitz – pack the world in your pocket!

Africa
Algeria
Kenya
Morocco
South Africa
Tunisia

Asia, Middle East
China
Egypt
Hong Kong
India
Indonesia
Japan
Jerusalem
Malaysia
Singapore
Sri Lanka
Taiwan
Thailand

Australasia
Australia
New Zealand
Sydney

Austria, Switzerland
Austrian Tyrol
Switzerland
Vienna

**Belgium,
The Netherlands**
Amsterdam
Brussels

British Isles
Channel Islands
Dublin
Ireland
London
Scotland

**Caribbean, Latin
America**
Bahamas
Bermuda
Cancún and Cozumel
Caribbean
French West Indies
Jamaica

Mexico
Mexico City/Acapulco
Puerto Rico
Rio de Janeiro
Southern Caribbean
Virgin Islands

**Central and
Eastern Europe**
Budapest
Hungary
Moscow and St Petersburg
Prague

France
Brittany
Châteaux of the Loire
Côte d'Azur
Dordogne
Euro Disney Resort
France
Normandy
Paris
Provence

Germany
Berlin
Munich
Rhine Valley

**Greece, Cyprus
and Turkey**
Athens
Corfu
Crete
Cyprus
Greek Islands
Istanbul
Rhodes
Turkey

Italy and Malta
Florence
Italy
Malta
Milan and the
Lakes
Naples
Rome
Sicily
Venice

North America
Alaska Cruise Guide
Boston
California
Canada
Disneyland and the
Theme Parks of
S. California
Florida
Greater Miami
Hawaii
Los Angeles
Montreal
New Orleans
New York
San Francisco
Toronto
USA
Walt Disney World
and Orlando
Washington

Portugal
Algarve
Lisbon
Madeira

Scandinavia
Copenhagen
Helsinki
Oslo and Bergen
Stockholm
Sweden

Spain
Barcelona
Canary Islands
Costa Blanca
Costa Brava
Costa del Sol
Costa Dorada and
Barcelona
Costa Dorada and
Tarragona
Ibiza and Formentera
Madrid
Mallorca and
Menorca
Seville

029/504 RP

Isabel Losada

100

Reasons to be Glad

summersdale

100 REASONS TO BE GLAD

Summersdale Publishers Ltd
46 West Street
Chichester
West Sussex
PO19 1RP
UK

www.summersdale.com

Printed and bound in Singapore

ISBN: 1-84024-548-4
ISBN: 978-1-84024-548-6

PHOTO CREDITS

Babies can swim when their mums take them to proper baby swimming classes.

Spiders build **amazing webs** and sometimes **drops of rain** get caught and the sun lights up the picture.

The Dalai Lama teaches kindness and we can practise practising it.

That sometimes **a bus comes along** just as you walk up to the bus stop.

That **Bill Watterson** created Calvin and Hobbs. And if you've never seen these books you get to read them for the first time.

Cats choose to live with human beings.

It's really easy to **make pancakes.**

The **chance to smile** at strangers everyday.

The sea.

Wild poppies.

That **Rodin decided** to study sculpture.

That if you wake up really early you can **hear the birds** celebrating the arrival of the day.

A chance to **dance.**

Mandela. His life choices. And the fact he wrote *Long Walk to Freedom* so we can read about them.

The smell of **freshly cut grass.**

It only takes 30 days to **form a new habit.**

Unexpected new friends.

That **Morecambe and Wise**
met each other.

GANDHI

HIS TRIUMPH CHANGED THE WORLD FOREVER.

WINNER OF 8 ACADEMY AWARDS®
INCLUDING 1982 BEST PICTURE

DVD
VIDEO

That **Richard Attenborough** chose to make a film about Gandhi and **kept going for ten years** till it was made.

That sometimes people **forgive and forget.**

Old friends who say 'I admire you' or anyone who says lovely things that they don't need to.

The right to **education.** (Mandela had to wait five years in prison for the right to read a book.)

That **J. K. Rowling** didn't listen when she was told 'You'll never make any money writing children's books.'

Pushbikes. The best invention ever. Good free transport and fun too. Especially at night with lights.

Tantric sex.

Voluntary Service Overseas.

www.vso.org.uk

Giraffes.

Going for **long walks** is free.

That we live after the invention of **washing machines.**

That **trees have blossoms** in springtime.

That dentists can give you **injections** before they drill your teeth.

That the **moon looks the same** as it did the first time we saw it.

Rumi's passionate poetry.

It feels so lovely when someone says **'Sorry.'**

Thich Nhat Hanh and his writings on the practices of Buddhism.

Labrador **dogs chasing balls**.

That some people **enjoy cooking** and making food taste fantastic.

There are **monks and nuns** all around the world who pray for us every day and believe that 'in some sort of mystical way it makes a difference'. (Sister Helen OHP)

That **Juliet Stevenson** became an actress and Anthony Minghella wrote *Truly Madly Deeply* for her.

Chocolate.

The books of **Mark Salzman**. Especially *True Notebooks*, in which he teaches creative writing to juvenile offenders in a youth detention centre.

Currant buns.

That Robin Williams is in **so many** films.

Friends who phone when they are sad and lost and **ask you to support them.**

That they made advertising **smoking illegal** and for all those who lobbied to make this happen.

That **Barbara Hepworth**

became a sculptor.

Big Ben and the two peace protestors who climbed up to ask for peace because they cared enough.

That **John Nash** succeeded as an architect.

Listening to the radio is cheap.

The still small **voice of calm.**

That we have a **National Health Service** and every day doctors save lives.

School friends who you want to **stay in touch** with.

Old-fashioned **spinning tops** that hum.

That **Bach** wrote some cello suites.

That **Gene Kelly** was cast in *Singin' in the Rain*.

That we have **equal rights** for the disabled and more and more ramps for wheelchairs. (A long way to go but it's coming.)

Lambs. (And the fact that some people don't eat them.)

Snowfall.

That someone found out that the potato was edible.

New pillows.

Sandals.

That we can go to Speakers' Corner and **say whatever we want.**

Anybody who ever **loved** us – even a little.

A teacher helped us learn to read.

Tenderness.

Public libraries.

That our eyes can see colour.

Beach huts.

That we have **four seasons**
and the weather is always changing
so we all appreciate a sunny day.

Shark protection.

www.sharktrust.org

That Cole **Porter** and George **Gershwin** wrote songs.

Candles. The state of Peace. And any contribution that we can make.

That we can always give ourselves **another chance.**

That we live in a **multi-cultural** society.

The choice to **stay in** when it rains or the choice to **go out** and get wet.

All the **tunes** and all the lyrics in *My Fair Lady*.

The extraordinary work of **Dame Judi Dench.**

Fountain pens.

Anyone we know who can play a musical instrument.

Edinburgh.

We can all make the **world** a better place.

Trees – any trees – all trees – from any angle.

Our **favourite film** ever.

Puddles and the right to jump in them.

Breathing deeply makes you feel good.

The Internet. And the joy of e-mail that doesn't interrupt people's lives.

The first person we think of who **makes us laugh**.

Sea horses.

The smell of freshly **ground coffee** or your five most favourite smells.

Coloured pencils.

A glass of water.

That there is relative **peace** in Northern Ireland.

That **Mother Teresa** looked after the dying and her community is all over the world – especially in Baghdad.

Re-incarnation may be true.

We can always **do something different.**

Toast.

Digital cameras. I don't have one yet but maybe one day I will.

That we can send **birthday cards** to our friends.

That we can **swear** if we want to.

That you can **write** your own list.

www.summersdale.com